ARCHERY
IN EARNEST

Roy Matthews MBE
and John Holden

THE CROWOOD PRESS

First published in 1985 by
THE CROWOOD PRESS
Ramsbury, Marlborough
Wiltshire SN8 2HE

British Library Cataloguing in Publication Data

Matthews, Roy
    Archery in earnest.
    1. Archery—Great Britain
    I. Title
    799.3'2'0941   GV1188.G7

    ISBN 0-946284-31-8

Acknowledgements

Our thanks go to everyone who helped with the book – there
are just too many names to mention. However, we owe a
special debt to:
Pauline Edwards
Mark Blenkarne
Steve Hallard
Les Howis and family, and staff, of Marksman Bows Ltd
Tony and Suzanne Preston of Perris Archery

Typeset by Quadraset Ltd, Midsomer Norton, Bath, Avon
Printed in Great Britain by Robert Hartnoll Ltd, Bodmin,
Cornwall

Contents

Foreword

The arrow appeared to float against the background of pale blue sky, its initial speed seemingly spent; just floating and getting smaller. Time was magnified and all that existed was me, and the gold disc on the target nearly a hundred yards away. The floating arrow made a beautiful curved arc between me and the target. I could see the bow toppling gently at the end of my outstretched arm, and the fingers of my right hand were limp and gently touching the back of my neck. I could still feel the almost ecstatic release of co-ordinated power from the muscles of my back and arms, the power that now belonged to that diminishing arrow.

The flight of that arrow was part of me, part of my freedom. At nearly two hundred feet per second it had left the bow, curved upwards, glinted a couple of times in the bright sunlight as it lost its first vibrations, then drifted slightly without a tremor as it absorbed the energy of the wind.

My body was frozen and time meant nothing, my mind only aware of the release of energy, my eye seeing the last seemingly faster flight of the arrow to the golden disc, my ears only hearing the low vibrant note of the bow.

Then the arrow struck. The strike was clear and magnified almost as if I could see the vibrations of the arrow as it gave its last remaining energy to the target. It had fulfilled its meaning for me as it pointed its fletchings back to me, not just from the gold disc, but from the inner gold disc, the ten-ring.

That link between me and the target started to fade when I heard the sharp distinctive noise coming back of the arrow hitting the target. There were other arrows in the target, more in the gold, the rest in the red ring around it, none more than a foot from the furthest.

My arms dropped and my hand went automatically to the now empty quiver. I heard the continual, irregular twang of many bows and the reflecting 'plonk' of arrows hitting the vast row of bright coloured targets. My head dropped gently forward as my shoulders relaxed, their strength no longer needed.

I wanted it to finish now, yet I wanted it to go on forever. Then I saw my white trousers and felt the tension go out of my knees. Between my feet I could see the coloured tape and a number on a disc, the same number below the target which was now part of me. As I raised my head I could see the other archers on the line and the gentle noise of people started to intrude.

As I walked away from the shooting line to cross the five metre line, the voices became more persistent but the words no clearer. There were too many languages; so, looking down I went to the bow rack and carefully replaced my bow. Many arrows had already been shot that day and many more would be shot; and my mind was still recording, calculating and analysing, so, for a moment more, I was still with that arrow.

Then I looked up and saw my team-mates and then my target companions. No words, just in the eyes and the faces. We understood. All of them had been into that world I had just left, and each shot made it easier to find the door again. We were the Master Bowmen.

Archery was always a combination of solitude, and self-discipline, a balance of understanding yourself and believing in yourself. That world on the shooting line was home but it was frightening. To be amongst the best archers in the world meant putting all of yourself into the effort, holding nothing back. Such nakedness is not acceptable to many; there is nowhere to run, nowhere to hide, only the performance is real. This solitude of self is not unique to archery, it exists for those who become the best in the cockpit of a racing-car, on the saddle of a racing cycle, on the hard road of a marathon runner. The archer is just using one of man's oldest tools. We still do not know how it all began . . . shooting bows and arrows.

Roy Matthews, MBE.

Introduction

I have tried to write about archery as I have experienced it. It may not be the same concept of shooting that is in the minds of other archers, but you will find that no matter what his personal interpretation may be, every top archer adheres to certain principles. Those principles are what I have in mind when describing technique and attitudes. Let me put some of those basic concepts to you now. They are the theme of the book and are repeated in many guises.

To hit the mark you need a good length of shot and good line. You also need a sound bow with well matched arrows. Please note the order of that list: personal skill must be the prime factor, equipment is secondary. Modern archery tackle covers a wide enough range of designs and performances to suit people of all shapes and sizes, all ages, all physical conditions.

Accuracy results from your shooting an arrow *in line* and with the right *length* or *height* of shot. Simply defined, *line* is the horizontal dispersion of shots across the target, *height* is the vertical spread. Where the two cross lies the gold. Thus, again on an elementary level of analysis, if you control the vertical and horizontal components of the shot, the arrow hits the middle.

Yes, this is a statement of the obvious. But it is so easy to forget these two fundamentals of archery. As your career progresses you will find that your mind fills with more and more knowledge about bows and arrows and how to shoot them. The difficult part of archery is not acquiring this knowledge, but retaining the wisdom to use it to your best advantage.

Aim for simplicity in your technique, and its measure of success will be the effect which you can produce on the line and height of the shot. This will not be an easy rule to follow; but then who said archery is easy? Shooting a bow is not like riding a bicycle or learning to swim. It demands the same co-ordination of mind and body but never becomes a learned habit. It never becomes pushed into the subconscious. There are times when the combination of mechanics and sensations seem impossible to comprehend let alone co-ordinate. It is then that an understanding of what is happening will prove far more useful than sheer knowledge. Awareness of self becomes the new dimension – and the vital one – to your shooting.

Once you have begun to shoot your bow and to aim at the mark, you will want to measure your progress in terms of scores. For target archers, the best assessment of competitive shooting is the FITA round. Traditionalists must forgive me for that! I too can wax lyrical about the English York and Hereford rounds, but for the sake of simplicity the FITA round will be the barometer of skill. And of course it is the one round familiar to archers world-wide.

What can the inexperienced archer expect to achieve in terms of score? With modern equipment – and not the most expensive – he is quite capable of scoring 1000 points for the FITA within two seasons of beginning to shoot. And 1100 points are quite possible soon after that. But remember, these levels are not yours of right. It is never said more truly than in archery that you get out of it only what you are willing to put in.

I can sit back and say that archery is a leisure sport – open air, blue sky, sun, the companionship of the archery club, and so on. Even so, archery is a competitive sport no matter whether you shoot field, clout, target or flight; and it is better to accept that scores are necessary to measure your skill against your neighbour's and to chart your personal progress.

Hard work alone does not necessarily produce good scores. (Although good scoring always needs working at.) Most important are:

1. Knowledge of what you and the bow are trying to do.
2. Awareness of what your body is actually doing.
3. Acceptance of what you are doing.
4. Faith in yourself.
5. Full commitment to what you wish to achieve.

The scores I have suggested are not meant for the impatient – those who need to know in detail the road before them, the fate which awaits. Archery does not demand such urgency. In fact, the opposite is nearer the truth. Let your personal development run at whatever speed you prefer. Your ultimate potential depends on your desire to learn and the speed at which you personally are able to progress. Age is no hindrance in this sport, so where is the rush? If you wish to dally among the entertaining, the challenging, the intriguing and the historical aspects of archery, then you are destined for endless pleasure.

To talk about archery is to describe the bow as well as the archer himself. The two are inseparable; the man with the bow becomes the archer. The modern bow is tailored to the man, and the man adjusts his technique to the bow. The two in unison are the complete archer. Modern archery equipment is as necessary to the development of the archer as to the intrinsic development of bows themselves. It does not detract from the purist or traditional values of the sport; it enhances them.

The greatest benefit offered by today's wide range of equipment is that anyone can shoot to an acceptable standard. Acceptable, that is, in that they can hit the target and group their arrows. This improvement in scoring power is only relative though. The best archers have always won and they always will. The true advantage of more consistent and accurate equipment is that the art of shooting the bow becomes paramount because the art of the bow itself has been reduced.

Traditionalists talk of the longbow, the yew bow of the fourteenth and fifteenth centuries. This is the weapon that kept the sport of archery alive in Europe and America to the present time. It is a very inefficient bow needing careful selection to find an acceptably accurate specimen. Its life can be short, and it calls for years of training to understand and shoot effectively. There was no alternative available in Europe until well into the twentieth century.

Eastern bowyery has been an art form for thousands of years, and the modern composite or recurved bow is a very sophisticated product of that illustrious line. I love my longbows for what they are; but is it not better by far to purchase a bow of known character and performance than to search for the elusive sweet shooting yew bow or to find six matched footed arrows from a half gross of wooden shafts? Of course it is. The very performance, reliability and accuracy of advanced equipment puts the emphasis where it truly belongs – on the archer himself.

I do not presume to tell you what you should do and what you cannot. Yet I find it so easy to let my words drift into a description of how you should shoot . . . a do-it-yourself instruction book. My true objective lies far from that. My personal experiences and achievements stem from the day I first shot an arrow in earnest, and if I describe how I found out about archery and how I decided on the important aspects, then I hope my thoughts will lead you to discover your own path to success. In the long run, though, you must reach your own conclusions. I cannot shoot your arrows for you any more than you can shoot mine, but between us perhaps we can make it a little easier. Remember, the ultimate requirement in archery is *confidence*. My definition of confidence is *knowledge* and *experience*. If you know how to do it right, and have done it right before, then you can do it again, and again . . . and again.

Roy Matthews, MBE

SECTION ONE
Roy Matthews MBE

1 First Shots

On first picking up a bow, beginners are immediately aware of the weapon's simplicity and its awkward feel. Few have not seen a bow before, in real life or on the screen, or read about archery. Yet to handle the bow and draw back its string is a far cry from the elegance associated with archery.

Those first attempts at shooting mould your attitude to the sport. Either you become fascinated by archery, or are scared off by the power and viciousness of what seems to be an uncontrollable weapon. And weapon it certainly is, not a toy to be played with. It is vitally important, therefore, to approach inauguration armed with some sense of purpose and understanding of the basics.

Your first bow may be a longbow or beginner's composite recurve, or even a modern compound. Whatever it is, there are three basic parts; bow, string and arrow. The trick of manipulation which you intend to carry out is to hold the bow in one hand, usually the left, fasten the arrow to the string, draw back, aim and let go. This summarises the fundamentals of archery and also highlights the problems of learning to shoot.

To shoot those first arrows and to experience the joy of archery, it is essential to be practiced enough to achieve a reasonable level of dexterity. But you have never even tried it before. So the first lesson to learn is that everyone has to start somewhere; nobody picks up a bow and shoots like a master.

From the technical point of view, you need a set of easy guidelines that at least allow you to pull back and release the arrow without hurting yourself or by-standers, and with an excellent chance of hitting the target rather than ploughing into the grass. This theme brings us to the first definition of target archery – the difference between bare-bow shooting and free-style. These terms are used in field archery rather than target shooting but are nonetheless relevant to the beginner.

At full draw, the target archer holds his bow upright with the drawing hand holding the string under and against the chin. The bow is aimed by means of a mechanical sight. This stance can only be achieved after considerable time and practice, and the object is to provide a very high level of consistency and accuracy.

However, the target stance is far from essential for shooting those first few arrows. Indeed, it is better to use a simpler style which shifts the emphasis towards pure enjoyment and away from the panic and physical strain of trying to co-ordinate fingers, chin, nose and sights. Bare-bow shooting, also known as instinctive shooting, is the perfect introduction to archery and naturally prepares the ground for a smooth switch to free-style techniques.

Strap an arm guard (bracer) to the forearm of your bow arm, and slip a finger tab onto your draw hand. Stand with your feet about shoulder width apart, toes pointing at right angles to the target which should be no more than ten to fifteen yards (or metres) distant. Hold the bow in the hand nearer the target (left for a right-handed archer) and clip an arrow onto the string.

Raise the bow in line with the target and hold the drawing hand between your face and the bow. Keep the drawing elbow high and in line with the arrow if possible. Hold the bow arm straight and set its shoulder as firmly as you can. Draw back the string and feel the weight of the bow push down the bow arm and into the shoulder. Let the top of the bow lean slightly away from you towards the right and keep the drawing hand snug against your right cheek. If your face is held fully towards the target with the head tipped slightly to one side – the same way as the bow – then the arrow can be seen to lie in a line from under the eye towards the target. The point, or pile, of the arrow appears to be several feet below the target's centre.

Hold the bow as steadily as you can at full draw, increase the drawing pressure a little . . . and relax your fingers off the string. The arrow will speed on its

Bare bow style is the most comfortable and natural way to begin shooting.

way. There is a fair chance that you will have hit the target, and without feeling any pain.

TARGET ARCHERY TECHNIQUE

The shooting style just described is the nearest you can get to purely instinctive, natural archery. Practised and refined it is a very satisfying way to shoot, the basis of the simplest forms of field shooting and bow-hunting. What quickly becomes apparent is the feeling of plenty of power in the shot but very little control. The first two or three shots hit close to the mark, yet it is hard to maintain tight groups. The obvious problem is lack of consistent aim.

Look at a target archer at full draw and now you understand why he stands in that seemingly rigid position with bow upright and drawing hand held tight under his chin. The stance is arranged with two functions in mind; aiming the bow, and controlling the power and speed of the arrow. Aiming is further improved by a bow sight which is adjustable for elevation and windage.

The drawing hand position is by far the most important difference between instinctive and target styles. The hand controls the string's location, which in turn fixes the distance between the arrow nock and the archer's aiming eye. An archer uses a fixed back sight and an adjustable foresight. Of the two, the foresight is the less important. Indeed, aiming itself is less critical to the making of an accurate shot than many inexperienced archers imagine. Of course it is important; and while developing your personal style you must pay attention to anchor, alignment and sighting. But certainly to begin with you will do better to put far more emphasis on letting go of the string. Therefore, let us break from this discussion on aiming and think about release.

LEARNING TO LET GO OF THE STRING

The release is the culmination of that sequence of steps you call your technique or style. I stress this because it is a common mistake to think of it as a separate, almost unrelated action. In fact, release is just one more stage in the flow from nocking the arrow to following through after the arrow leaves the bow, and its success is highly dependent on how you build up to it, and what you do afterwards.

Stance

The most comfortable stance is with feet shoulder width apart and body weight equally balanced. Stand tall with the spine as straight as possible. Look over your shoulder at the target to remind yourself how your head will be aligned at full draw.

Precise anchoring is the target archer's method of ensuring exact arrow alignment.

Bow hand

Fingers should curl around the grip in a loose, natural manner. The back of the wrist must be straight and held firm when the pressure of the bow pushes into the hand. The wrist must not drop or cock backwards when the bow is drawn. Some form of bow sling is advisable right from the start so that you do not develop the bad habit of grabbing the bow when you release the string.

String fingers

The fingers, covered by the tab, should hold the string in the first crease of the first three fingers; index finger above the nock, second and third below. At this stage the second joints can be curled a little since they will

Basic technique 2 – bow shoulder/arm position and the start of the draw.

automatically straighten as the string is drawn. The draw hand wrist should be relaxed right from the start.

Drawing

The main fulcrum for the shot is the *bow shoulder*. Lift both hands in line with the target, bow arm extended and string drawn a few inches. Set the bow shoulder *down* and *in line* with the shoulders. This is your pre-draw or first draw position.

Draw the string back. Your draw wrist should be cocked outward at the start of tension and, if it really is as relaxed as it should be, will straighten itself as the pressure increases. Complete the draw by placing your index finger along the jaw with the string pulled back into the chin.

Holding

The front shoulder should not have moved during the

Basic technique 1 – stance and preparation.

draw, and your body should still be standing tall with the spine straight. If you have drawn the string correctly, the drawing elbow should feel as if it is well behind your head with the string held in a hook formed by your fingers.

At this stage the unnatural aspects of shooting are evident. Take the bow shoulder for example. In our everyday lives we tend to be idle with our bodies, using bone joints, often in a hyper-extended position, to shape our posture. When a load must be resisted at arm's length, it feels much more comfortable and easier if the elbow and shoulder joints are locked.

When we stand with the weight of a fully drawn bow pressing down the length of the arm, we lose the feeling of solidarity and control if the bow is supported by muscles. The tendency is to lock the joints and let the bones take the strain off those hard-worked muscles.

Basic technique 4 – release and follow through.

If you intend to hold and aim a bow correctly, you must condition your muscles to share the strain. Any temptation to allow the shoulder to rise towards the neck or to collapse across the chest must be resisted. Similarly, the elbow of the bow arm must be held so that it does not protrude into the string's path. Hyper-extended, locked elbow is the main cause of self-injury during an archer's early training. The risk is higher with females due to the greater natural flexion of the joint.

The string hand also feels awkward at full draw. From birth we have an instinctive reaction to grip an object harder the more force we wish to exert. Fingers and thumb naturally curl to form a fist, especially when we grip a slender article. But to draw the string with any chance of a controlled release, fingers must be allowed to extend as hooks with only the last joints supporting the weight.

It is during this hold position that we make the first rudimentary attempts at aiming. Remember that the

Basic technique 3 – anchor, holding and aiming.

back sight – the anchor – is more important than the bow-sight position and must be mastered first. The anchor position depends upon personal preference and on the archer's physique. The priorities are comfort and consistency. The aiming eye sees the string as a blurred image aligned with the side of the bow or some other definite reference point; and the anchor establishes a precise vertical reference point for the shot's elevation. Within those two parameters lies considerable scope for experiment and variation, as will be seen later.

Releasing

Much has been written about releasing, yet there is still great confusion in the ranks of archers. Later in the book is a more detailed analysis, but for now it can adequately be described in the following manner.

Release is controlled by the position you are in *before* it happens, and what you do with your body *after* it happens. By deciding on what you intend to do afterwards, you also control the condition that exists beforehand. If this sounds complicated and vague, be patient, and keep uppermost in your mind that a good release cannot be properly controlled by the conscious mind forcing the fingers to let go. Think more along the lines of it being just another step in the whole shooting sequence rather than a deliberate, conscious action. Nor is it the culmination of the shot or even its focal point.

However, as a beginner you need some deliberate method of actually sending the arrow on its way. Try this simple introduction to the main elements of technique.

1. When at full draw, with the bow arm reaching towards the target and the drawing elbow well behind your head, mentally think about forming a fist with the empty hand, behind the neck. Then do it. The fingers will relax and allow the string to accelerate forward with least interference. The string pushes your relaxed fingers out of the way.
2. When you are familiar with the concept of making a fist, add the mental image of lifting the bow hand as the string is released.
3. The third ingredient is introduced after the first two are happening regularly. As the bow hand appears to be lifted, feel that you are tilting the bow forward. The top limb tips in line with the target.

This simple system of three actions, learned during your very first days of shooting the bow, is the foundation of the muscular requirements of a good technique, which can be summarised as:

1. Use of shoulders to their full power.
2. Relaxation of the drawing forearm.
3. Maintaining a solid front shoulder.
4. Keeping the bow wrist strong and firm.

If you are a naturally fast learner, or have competent archers to guide you, style and accuracy should develop quite quickly. Much depends on your level of co-ordination. However, speed of learning is no measure of how good an archer you will be in the long run. The secret is to progress at a comfortable pace so that your shooting develops the flow and consistency necessary to shoot tight groups from the first end to the last of a long tournament. Ultimate control of your shooting comes only from awareness of what your body is actually doing. You must serve a full apprenticeship . . . and that takes time as well as practice.

2 Development of Technique (1)

FACTORS THAT PRODUCE LINE IN THE SHOT

Even the most cursory inspection of the shooting line highlights the wide range of physiques and styles that archers may develop. This is equally true of a local club event as of an international championship or even the Olympic Games, and it demonstrates the practicality of archery for all.

There is no clearly definable ideal archery physique, yet certain characteristics are advantageous while others are less than perfect. An obvious example is the long-limbed, undeveloped youth who must shoot a long arrow from a long bow, but who lacks the muscular strength to control a bow of optimum draw weight. In general though, if a line of good archers is observed more closely, certain common factors are apparent.

Stance

Although the top half of the body (arms and shoulder girdle) is the archer's power house, the lower body is the platform which gives each shot its stability and consistency. How you stand is the first physical preparation for the shot.

The most common, and usually the most comfortable position is with your feet just less than shoulder width apart and both at right angles to the line of shot. This causes the least skeletal distortion and is particularly beneficial to the spinal column. Hips and shoulders are square to the target; raising the arms sideways develops your first sense of line.

This position suits many archers, me included, but for the more extreme of build some departure from square can be advantageous and more comfortable. Those archers with a larger bulk may find the open stance provides better upper body clearance for both bow arm and string. An open stance is when the hips are turned slightly towards the target, the position being found by moving the foot nearest to the target a little to the rear. The body then faces a point somewhat in front of the shooting line rather than straight along it.

A slightly-built archer with smaller bone structure and less weight often feels unstable in the square stance, particularly at full draw. This is possibly due to excessive tension in the muscles which generates an up-and-down effect within the slimmer skeleton instead of the powerful cross-bracing that naturally occurs in those of broader, heavier build.

Youngsters are at an obvious disadvantage, as can be seen by the contortions that develop as they attempt to inject power into their shots. And although women in general have less trouble with stance due to their wider hips, there are problems with string clearance for those with well developed busts.

Whatever the reason may be, if standing square makes you feel unstable or does not provide adequate string clearance, do experiment with an open stance – up to 45 degrees to the shooting line if necessary. Now it takes a very pronounced spinal twist to bring your shoulders back into line with the target, but the technique gives a very stable feeling to the whole body, and if properly held does assist in keeping the draw elbow well back and in line with the arrow.

It must be stressed, however, that spinal torsion relies upon bone joints to hold your body steady, therefore it detracts from the ideal technique of holding with a balanced combination of bone and muscle. Be sure there is no feeling of stress, otherwise your bone joints can be damaged by the heavy isometric loads imposed during shooting.

The body, it must be understood, should be in the 'tall' position at all times. The above remarks about

Developing line 1 – preparing the shot.

archers, champions in particular. If you want to analyse and model yourself on your hero, by all means go ahead, but sensibly. We all have fantasies, but in archery you need to be a little more realistic. It is usually more rewarding to base yourself on a good archer of the same sex who is similar in age and build.

Preparing to draw

From the start of drawing to the climax of release, elapsed time is between five and ten seconds – a very short period in which to complete a complex series of actions and with no time for confused thinking. It is essential from now on that you develop a sense of sequence into your actions so that your thoughts run to a pattern. Remember that your mind should direct your body *through* all of the actions; it should not be

Developing line 2 – bow shoulder in place and draw elbow moving back.

spinal twist mean just that: under no circumstances allow yourself to sag until the joints of the spine, hips and legs collapse into the 'locked' state. Only when you stand upright does body weight flow correctly down the skeletal system.

Another variation on basic stance concerns the proportion of weight on each foot. There is an instinctive desire to lean back and concentrate your weight on the back foot as the bow comes to full draw (this will be discussed later) and it may be better to alter your foot spacing to give greater control. Some archers spread their feet wide apart for greater inherent stability, which sometimes reduces the problem. Others shift their feet close together because then any tendency to lean backwards immediately results in a strong sensation of imbalance. Thus, control and feedback are strongly emphasised and you are far less likely to develop long-term bad habits.

A final observation on stance – and indeed on overall styles – concerns the danger of blindly copying other concerned with mentally checking on the body's condition *after* the action is made.

That last point bears repetition. If the action of drawing is carried out as a learned response, then the state of the bone structure and muscles at full draw will need to be checked and perhaps readjusted before you attempt to aim and let go. This way of shooting is painful and difficult.

To aid your development of the right sequence and mental approach, I will go through the actions in the order in which they should be carried out, starting with the hands. The *bow hand* is not required to grip the handle of a modern composite bow. A loose grip is essential if the bow is to react, or recoil, without hindrance. Instead, think of the bow hand as a carefully positioned cushion between the bow arm and the bow itself.

Developing line 4 – line is maintained after release.

Developing line 3 – elbow behind head. Bow weight has transferred from arms to back.

The problem with the bow hand is its construction. Depending on the size of the archer's hand, its position on the bow handle can vary in the vertical plane to alter the pressure point between bow grip and palm. This vertical angle is referred to as low, medium or high grip. The precise position is one of personal choice, though certain rules do apply.

The pressure of the bow is most effectively taken on the pad of muscle at the base of the thumb, between thumb and first finger. The load must not be taken on the thumb itself, or on the heel of the palm. The object is to form a controlled line of pressure along the forearm. Any adjustment needed to alter the clearance between string path and arm should be made by rotating the wrist around that point of pressure running into the palm. The overall position of your bow hand can easily be judged by noting the angle that the knuckles make to the vertical. An angle of 45 degrees is a good starting point for experiment. Once the hand and wrist are positioned correctly, no movement should be allowed. Your bow wrist must be firm throughout the shot.

The *drawing hand* is simply a pulling unit. The position of the fingers on the string is usually called the lock on the string. Target archers use one finger above the arrow and two below. Field archers employ a variety of positions when they shoot without a bow sight. The method is known as string walking and controls aiming and elevation; but whatever the relationship between arrow and finger location on the string, the drawing hand's basic action is always constant – and the same as for target work.

In preparation for the draw, the hand is relaxed or cupped with the string positioned in the first joint (that

is, the joint closest to the fingertip). The second joint of each finger will flex individually to keep the creases of the first joint all in line with the string. Beginners find it difficult to keep the third finger in position and taking its full share of the load. It will strengthen with practice – although it will be the one that hurts the most.

Since Roger Ascham wrote about drawing in *Toxophilus* (published in 1545), nobody has better described the condition of an archer's fingers. "And when a man shooteth, the might of his shot lieth on the foremost finger and on the ringman (third finger); for the middle finger which is longest, like a lubber, starteth back, and beareth no weight of the string in a

Draw elbow sling in action.

manner at all . . . and for sure loosing, the foremost finger is most apt, because it holdeth best.''

There have been good shooters who dispensed with the first finger, leaving it to lie alongside the string with no bend at all, but they were very, very few. Adjusting the bend of the finger joints to form a hook can only be a compromise and at times may seem an impossible task when it comes to letting go of the string. But the first finger not only takes its full share of the weight, it also acts as the drawing hand's locator against the face to form the back sight. However, at this stage of the shot the drawing hand is simply hooked onto the string. Its true role will develop when the bow is drawn and released.

DRAWING

Since the key to good archery is the making of powerful, in-line shots, it helps if we think back from the release to understand the importance of how a bow is drawn.

Release is the result of how the bow is held at full draw. The condition of the body at full draw, in turn, is the result of how the bow was drawn. So, from the moment the string starts moving back, we are affecting the way the arrow will leave the string. This all seems very obvious when written down, but when you actually shoot an arrow there is a temptation to 'sort it all out at full draw'. Possible of course, but not the easiest way.

When recurved composite bows were slender one-piece weapons and light in hand, it was normal practice to raise the bow higher than the head and lower it to the sighting line during the draw. The weight of a fully equipped modern take-down can be 5lb (2·3kg) or more, and with that much to control it makes more sense to cut movement to a minimum.

The action of drawing the string to form the line of a shot can now be thought of as three stages.

1. The string is drawn a few inches to settle the weight of the bow into the hand, and the string into the draw fingers.
2. The bow is raised to its sighting plane and the string is drawn back to two-thirds or three-quarters of the full arrow length to prepare the body for the full draw weight of the bow.
3. The bow is fully drawn, the drawing hand comes to anchor, and the line of the shot is fully developed. The entire sequence is known as setting up the shot.

Throughout the draw, the *fulcrum* of the line is the *front*, or *bow shoulder*. When you start to draw the string, the drawing arm lies across your body and the bow's weight is mostly on your arms. As draw length and weight increase, this load must be transferred on to the back, and the resulting rotation of the rear arm shoulder blade must *pivot* on that front shoulder. The final movement, after the rear shoulder blade is in position, is to pull your draw elbow back *behind* your head, in line with the arrow.

The second fulcrum of the line is the wrist of the *drawing hand*, which should be in line with the arrow from the very beginning of the draw. As the rear elbow moves behind your head, the forearm acts as an inert linkage between the wrist (which is already in line) and the rear elbow. The final act of drawing completes the line of the shot from the front hand, through the length of the arrow and wrist, to finish at the rear elbow held well back behind the head.

A drawing hook is a most useful device to help you feel the sensation of drawing correctly and developing line. The photograph shows how easy it is to simulate the correct draw action by effectively by-passing fingers and forearm with a leather cup hooked over the draw elbow.

To use the hook, adjust the cord between the cup and the string to the correct length, slide the cup onto your elbow and clip the cord just below the nocking point. Set and hold your front shoulder. Raise the bow as for normal shooting, but take the full weight on your drawing elbow. Fingers and forearm are perfectly relaxed. At full draw the string can be brought into correct facial alignment solely by the position of your elbow. Practise your drawing sequence, and learn to feel how the weight transfers to and is held through the shoulders as full draw approaches. Sense the development and holding of line as well.

ANCHORING

The final position of the archer's drawing hand is usually termed anchor point, but this description has fallen into disrepute in some coaching quarters. Objections arise from the impression of a rigid, immobile clamping of the hand against the face. This is utterly wrong; however, I still prefer to use the term anchor point because I see it as the dynamic straining under load which is conveyed by a picture of a ship held at anchor in a tide race.

Your anchor must be capable of locating the string, and hence the rear of the arrow, in the same position relative to the bow every shot. This requires both line (left and right) and height. Line is easier to learn because the string can be seen as a blurred image that is lined up with the edge of the bow handle or with the

2 – Predraw and establishing initial aiming line.

COMPOSITE FORM DEMONSTRATED BY PAULINE EDWARDS
1 – Stance and preparation.

sight bar itself.

Vertical location is more difficult to establish because of the required contact with your face. The traditional location for FITA target shooting is with the top finger along and under the jaw bone, and with the string pulled into the centre of the chin. Precise alignment demands that the head be tilted slightly away from vertical to bring the aiming eye over the line of the arrow.

Centre anchoring is by no means the best or only way to do it. Side-of-face anchor is popular – here the top finger still lies against the jaw bone, but the string is drawn further back, directly under the aiming eye and in contact with the side of the face. This anchor point leads to a much more relaxed head position and can be a major advantage to spectacle wearers who now can look through the centre of the lens.

If you are shooting to more relaxed rules which allow peep sights in the string, the problems of lining up the shot and the anchor point are much less of a com-

*3 – Final draw and anchor. Note the rear elbow
position and the use of back muscles.*

as a flow. This harmony between what is *thought* and what is *felt* is one of archery's basic concepts and will arise again in later chapters.

So, to recap. Beginning with *stance* and standing tall, you draw a few inches to settle bow grip and string fingers. The bow is raised to the *aiming line* of the sight, and front shoulder settles in response to the *pre-draw*. The front shoulder is held down by your back muscles, and its line is checked against the drawing hand wrist. The wrist appears to be turned inwards (as you look down on it), and the distance between wrist and bow shoulder will be about equal to the length of thumb were it outstretched.

The *final draw* is a smooth movement which brings the drawing elbow back in line with the arrow, pivoting on the *draw wrist* as the front shoulder takes the full weight of the bow. The *anchor* is found first

promise. The relationship between peep sight and arrow are fixed throughout the shot. Aiming is reduced to two visible references, and the archer's main task is simplified so that he can pay more attention to power and good release.

THE COMPOSITE PATTERN OF LINE DEVELOPMENT

I have deliberately discussed the start and end of the draw in some detail since they represent two fixed points in what is a complex action involving the entire upper body. The object at this stage is still to establish the *line of shot*, and the best way to do that is by developing a drawing sequence that utilises the simplest of muscle actions; or more precisely, the least number of muscles.

These actions are controlled mentally as a series of steps, but the transition of one to the next must be felt

4 – Powerful release and follow through with line maintained.

Line and consistent power – the secret of accurate shooting.

with the *string picture* and physically by touching the chin. The whole weight of the bow is now felt between the front arm and shoulder, and the rear elbow. Then the anchor is finally completed as the top finger makes vertical contact with the jaw.

The head is held steady during the action of drawing, but the neck muscles are relaxed to allow movement of the head so that you can settle into your anchor without losing draw length. The bow weight is held between the firmness of the front end and the position of the draw elbow.

Setting up a shot with a sense of a sequence, each step leading naturally to the next, helps considerably with this concept of *line*. You can feel it developing in the whole body: the balancing of body weight on the feet; the settling of your hips; the solid fulcrum of the front shoulder; the bow and string hand/finger locations; the extension between the front arm and rear elbow as the draw progresses, and the smooth transfer of weight onto your back. This controlled sequence is a vital foundation for the ultimate act of releasing the string down the right *line* with consistent *power*, wherein lies the secret of accurate shooting.

3 Development of Technique (2)

FACTORS THAT PRODUCE POWER IN THE SHOT

So far we have considered the shot sequence as a mechanical act. It must be so in order to develop the correct position and alignment of the archer's bone structure. The *power* of the shot will build up from the muscles, and culminates in the controlled release of body energy into the bowstring.

String release is the climax of a shot and appears effortless when performed with skill; yet it is always so difficult to describe and teach. Roger Ascham again: "it may be perceived better in a man's mind when it is done, than seen with a man's eyes when it is doing." A

Most leading archers use the space between shots to mentally rehearse their routine.

succinct, accurate, but perhaps not very helpful observation. Even though high-speed cameras provide an insight into the departure of bowstring from the archer's fingers, the true nature of the release *action* is not defined, nor the thoughts described.

I shall make a definition, then discuss its implications. The release is the *moment between* holding at full draw and making the follow through. It can be seen between the two, but neither after the one, nor before the other. Thus, we are talking about the release as a *reaction* rather than as an *action*.

The action which an archer does at full draw is to prepare for the follow through. The control of arrow flight will thus be a result of a transition from 'now you have the string in your fingers' to 'now you do not'.

Let us first consider the condition we wish to achieve after release. We want the bow to punch toward the

2. Take one deep breath as you settle your fingers into the string.

aiming mark, the drawing arm to travel directly away from the bow's path. We want to feel relaxed with no jerky movements, to maintain our balance and not be out of breath. We want to enjoy releasing the arrow and feeling the bow's power.

Breathing

Going back to the setting up of line, we can now begin to understand the translation to power. Controlled breathing is the first factor. The body needs oxygen, and it needs it at the right time. Archers have a disadvantage in that any form of breathing at the climax of a shot will distort the act of aiming. A rhythm becomes essential, and a useful sequence that fits the set-up of a shot is this:

1. Shallow breaths between shots.
2. One deep breath as the bow is drawn to settle the

POWER AND BREATHING
1. Relax and breathe easily between shots.

3. Exhale as the bow rises.

string fingers.
3. Exhale as the bow rises to aiming position.
4. Inhale to half or three-quarters capacity as the arrow is drawn to full length.
5. Let the lungs exhale naturally as release occurs.

Muscle control

The next factor is muscle control. You can only feel relaxed after the shot if the muscles not required for drawing the bow are relaxed at full draw. Some tension in the legs is necessary, especially when you shoot in the wind; but you must resist the temptation to brace your knees back against the joints. The main focus of body posture should come from your stomach muscles which must be held firm throughout the shot. The Chinese have a concept called *Chi* in which the focus of all our emotions and thoughts is at a spot a few centimetres below the navel. It has valid connections with archery.

The sensation of 'standing tall' must be retained throughout, and is best described as a feeling rather than a deliberate clenching of muscles to maintain posture. The upper body is the powerhouse, and its sensations are concentrated on the *balance* between the bow's pressure against the front hand and the pull of the rear elbow. You are aware of the bow arm through the solidness of the shoulder and the wrist's firmness. The bow arm elbow is extended but not locked. The feeling is one of *extension*; and only the muscles of the upper arm contribute towards the necessary control. The bow handle is not gripped, thus the forearm is relaxed.

The real power of the upper body is felt across the back. If the actions of line development are correct, the shoulder blade of the drawing arm is almost as flat as

4. Inhale as line and power develop.

5. *Exhale naturally during release and follow through.*

the front shoulder blade. The powerful muscles of the upper back hold the entire shoulder girdle in line with the bow arm.

The forearm of the drawing arm is felt as a link connecting elbow to wrist, and since no gripping action is required here either, the forearm muscles are relaxed. The whole weight of the drawn bow is felt through the muscles of the back, not on the arms.

Follow through

The final factor is the follow through. It is the ultimate awareness of how you intend to feel afterwards that triggers the release itself. The aim has been secondary so far, but now dominates because the shot feels well controlled. The sight is held on the centre of the mark not by a pushing action but by a reaching sensation of the whole bow arm. The drawing hand which lies close to the neck will remain close as the string leaves the fingers. It is relaxed; and being controlled by the rear elbow's pulling action will finish behind the neck as the recoiling drawing unit takes it back smoothly and undisturbed.

The follow through has a curious sensation of rotation around the axis of the arrow. The bow hand has a slight feeling of 'aiming' with the thumb, which lifts and holds the bow during release. The drawing wrist has a more definite sensation of rotating to bring the back of the wrist to face upwards. These two reactions are very different in degree, and they occur in opposite directions of rotation.

In producing the shot's power, then, we have moved quite clearly from the *mechanical positioning* of bones to the *sensations* arising from muscle action; the change is predominantly from *action* to *reaction*. I have found that the more I develop this concept of line and power, the clearer becomes the transition from that initial drawing-and-holding to holding-and-loosing.

The first holding is a result of preparations, the second holding is actually the beginning of release. They may look the same, but the mind sees them as being different. The concept of the whole shot is realised only during that second phase, which explains why it is so hard to come to terms with the mental side of shooting. When champion archers say that good shooting is mostly a mental exercise, this is the area to which they refer. The development of your personal mental image of a complete shot is not only vitally important but also difficult. Ultimately, it represents the 7th Dan of archery – a striving for the impossible.

4 The Gap

THE PROBLEM

To the onlooker an archer at full draw can appear statuesque – tall, calm, and powerful; a Greek statue. To the archer those few seconds at full draw can be a turmoil of thoughts, or they can be the culmination of co-ordination and control. It is this contrast of minimum action when making maximum effort which interests me most. It is also the facet of shooting which is most difficult to define.

Looking for comparisons in other sports is difficult since all physical, non-opponent projectile sports seem to build up momentum so that the climax of the effort occurs at the point of maximum action. Obvious examples are bowling, golf, shot-putting, javelin-throwing and snooker. The archer needs to produce a consistent, explosive release of the string at the point of maximum stillness. The archer's body may appear to have stillness but the effort, the physical effort, is only maintained by disciplined mental control of the body.

The more shooting one does and hopefully the better one shoots, the more this enigma becomes apparent. The greater the calmness of the body, the greater the stillness, the more active the mind becomes. The thoughts race through the mind, often in some frantic pattern, fed by the nerves of the body in its climax of effort. Surely there is no better example, no better demonstration, that the mind should be at one with the body?

This state of mind, when the archer is actually making the shot, is not always the same, particularly as the archer's shooting career develops.

The early stages of learning how to shoot are characterised by the mental effort of trying to learn a new activity, a new skill. The mind has too much to order, to control, to check through; and the body is always the first to fail; the muscles shake and lack strength.

The state of mind of the experienced archer is a complete reversal of that of the novice. Now the body is trained, the muscles strong and in good tone. The sequence of actions has become habit, and the making of the shot becomes a learned motor-skill, like riding a bicycle. So many things are done by the body without conscious thought, and so the concept appears attainable of becoming the perfect repetitive archer. But the mind, the conscious mind, cannot learn these habits. It cannot submerge itself in the warmth of sensations alone, as the body has done. The mind, the conscious mind, is continually aware; it is constantly monitoring what the body is doing.

Let me describe the climax of the shot, that moment before the letting go of the string. The sight is on the gold. The arrow is drawn almost to the full length, only a fraction of an inch remains under the clicker. The physical effort of holding the bow at full draw is felt as a tremendous load upon the shoulders, the back, the arms, the fingers. An extension of that fraction of an inch on the draw length will release the clicker, the fingers can release the string, and the arrow can leave the bow. But, at this moment of maximum effort, what thoughts are in the mind, what thoughts should be in the mind?

One moment you are concentrating on building up the shot, with an awareness of what you are doing, until you are at full draw ready for the release. The next thing to happen will be the follow through as the arrow leaves the bow. During my years of shooting, I must have stood a thousand times waiting for the string to explode from my fingers as the arrow sped on its way, and I believe that mentally there is a *gap* between my thoughts at full draw, before the release, and the follow through after the release.

There can be a mental gap in the flow of our conscious thoughts and an understanding of this situation is crucial to the full understanding of making the shot. Let me describe this concept by example. You can be standing on the line, ready to make the shot as well as you are likely to on that day, the sight is smack in the

ROY MATTHEWS' COMPOSITE FORM
1. Predraw and initial aim. Setting bow shoulder.

middle . . . and then the little voices are heard in the head, and the doubts about the shot start to creep in; the wrong thoughts are entering the mind.

It is as if the thoughts creep into an empty space. There was nothing happening in the mind, so the thoughts appear to fill it. The mind cannot be blank while it is still conscious, so if there is something to think about and to occupy the mind then these other thoughts will not intrude. This situation is not always recognisable because when you are fit and strong and the shots are confidently made, then you build up the shot, have a good aim, and you pass straight across into the follow through. It is like an electric current. The flow of mental control has simply arced across the gap. No break. The shot was one continuous flow of mental and physical effort. The problem was, how could I stay in that flow of controlled effort, that rhythm, arrow after arrow, round after round?

THE ANALYSIS

The answer seemed to lie in separating the unconscious link between the mind and the body at the moment of truth because 'letting it happen', in the context of Timothy Gallwey's *Inner Game*, seemed to lead inexorably to 'nothing happening'.

One technique, one of many I might add, was based on the assumption that if movement was required to draw the arrow through the clicker, then movement there shall be. The hold at aim should be a 'don't stop' situation, starting from a good half inch of arrow under the clicker. All the requirements of shoulder posture, arm alignment, muscle loading and, of course, aiming, would be carried out as a learned response, a habit, while the mind concentrated on this backward draw, and forward pressure. Plenty to occupy the mind; no clocks involved here, no metronome of fear to blank the mind. Work to be done and a clicker to mark the climax.

It works. It is the haven of success for many a good scoring archer, but when the effort became too great, the arrow too long, a doubt appeared again almost like a feeling of guilt. There was no calmness, only physical effort. Another attempt at the singularity of concentration was based on the sight, on the aim. This concept is well researched and well documented, it is a variation on the 'let it happen' approach, and is one of the fundamentals of Zen in archery.

The problem with such a simplistic approach is the use of the clicker. It works as a technique when the arrow is resting free on the bow, then the conflict occurs between holding the length and holding the sight on the mark. The eye triggers the release from the image of the sight-pin on the target. Mind you, this aiming thing is much overrated in archery. If the sight is held rigid, as it appears to the eye, locked in the centre of the gold and yet the arrows group within only two colours of the gold, what was the significance of the aim as a major contribution to the shot? Another enigma perhaps? This technique works, but let me describe just one of the various failures.

2. *Developing line.*

3. Drawing to length.

4. Anchor and power.

5. *Extension and release.*

6. *Moving into follow through.*

The hold is strong, the aim is with the sight-pin dead centre, the line seems strong and true, and the clock keeps ticking away, deep inside. The hold seems harder but the sight stays in the middle. The tension comes off the back onto the arms, and effort is made to draw the arrow to the length and the loose becomes a tense, ungainly jerk. Then back I am to dumping arrows into that dustbin of FITA Stars . . . low left for a right-handed archer (low right for left-handers!)

THE CONCLUSION

The truth was that the mind has to be at one with the body. There was no achievement to be obtained in confusing physical movement with the dynamic calm which I was seeking, any more than mental control could be gained by staring inactively at the elusive gold. The shot had to be a complete thing. The mind had to be aware of the whole shot; me, and the bow, and the arrow. The key word in this concept was *aware*. Conscious of what was happening to me and conscious of what I was doing to make it happen.

Awareness is an abstract expression which is communicated through the feelings which you experience through the senses and nerves of your body. So now I was seeing my problem in the simplistic way that I had been seeking. What becomes clearer to me was that

7. *Follow through and line held until arrow hits.*

The bow wrist is FIRM although the bow arm is RELAXED.

when thinking about the whole shot there was not enough time to form complete thoughts which were recording my total awareness.

I may teach myself the individual parts, the actions, that make up the shot, by describing the detail in sentences; the front shoulder should be held so . . . the body posture should be so . . . the fingers should be on the string so . . . and so on. But when I made the shot there was no time for sentences, the arrow had to go. There was not enough time for sentences, there was only time for *words*. Words that described how I felt.

Now I knew what I was trying to do. Now I could simplify my concept of the shot. Not simplify what I had to do to make the shot, but simplify what I *thought* I had to do. What was I trying to achieve when I shot the arrow? Answer: hit the middle of the gold. If I draw a line vertically through the gold then that is the *line* of

the shot. If I draw a line horizontally through the gold that is the *height* of the shot. Where the two lines cross is the hit I wish to make. Height is a non-active word. The word which meant something to me was *power*. So now I had two words to control the shot: *line* and *power*.

What I could now see, in my mind, was the multitude of physical actions which all contributed to the concept of *line*. I could also feel, in my whole body, the muscular effort which produced the *power*.

How to shoot an arrow was not my problem. Like a thousand other archers I knew how to shoot. The details, like the body posture which suited me, from the width apart of my feet, to the shape of my spine; how I held the string and how my hand held the bow; the way I set my front shoulder, the drawing of the bow and the line of the drawing elbow. These were not a problem to me because I had shot enough perfect ends, from 90 metres down, to be confident that I had been able to put it all together repeatedly, consistently, for at least six shots!

What I could do was put all those into the box called *line* which controlled the line, and all those which controlled the power of the shot into the box called *power*. Now I could fill my gap with just two words. *Line* dominated the thoughts from the start of the shot, then *power* became dominant for the last part. Both words were continually in my mind.

At this stage I have to admit to a certain smugness. I had been searching so long for a secret, a simple answer to the complexity of shooting, and a simple answer I thought I had found. Archery is not easy, nor simple. Archery is difficult and it hurts. These two words had achieved for me a better control over the shots and also better scores, but there was still a feeling missing. When shooting well and the shots were flowing to a rhythm I always felt relaxed, a sort of physical relaxation.

The third word which should be with *line* and *power* was *relax*, but this always seems a contradiction. Muscular tension was the basis of the power of the shot so that the problem was that if relaxation was also essential to the shot, what had to be relaxed? Digging back into my personal store of techniques, the box-rooms of experience, I tried to think simply of my body when I shot, and tried to recall and to recognise those relaxed, easy, shots.

The conclusion which I came to was that I relaxed my forearms at the final stage of the shot, and then the whole sensation was one of flowing controlled power. Because I am thinking about a sensation I can only describe what I feel in the context of the shot. At the stage of drawing I start to build up the concept of *line*, starting with the front shoulder. As the final draw results then the *power* has developed from the position of the back elbow and the line of the shoulders. The draw length is to half pile under the clicker. The aim is centre on the gold and the *power* is holding the *line*. At this stage I am conscious of physically relaxing the forearms, not the front wrist, and the desired extension takes place. The arrow is through the clicker and I am only aware of the follow through . . . of where the hands have moved to.

What is both frightening, but ecstatic, is that there is a feeling of insecurity. The thoughts seem wrong in the sense that I have been holding the sight firm in the centre of the gold, holding a full, powerful length, and then relaxing what I thought was keeping everything where it should be. As the scores of the arrow strikes improved so did my confidence, and a feeling develops of a tremendous sensation of controlled power.

The immediate effect was to have a much simpler concept of the whole shot. I can 'see' the shot which I am making in terms of *LINE – POWER – RELAXATION*. Shooting the bow is no easier, it is just more complete in my mind. There are days when to achieve line seems almost too difficult, and days when power is unattainable; but there is almost no feeling of failure. The task is always the same: to put it all together into the one shot.

What seems to make the shot simpler is that since I can 'see' it as a complete thing, I only have to be aware of what is 'missing'. I start with a full list – in my three boxes – and I 'see' what is missing from line, and what is missing from power. Relaxation is discussed in more detail in the next chapter but, at this point, I hope that the enigma of maximum effort with minimum action is less of a mystery. What I found is that it is possible to make judgements after each arrow with no reference to right or wrong, for that is no longer relevant, but judgements which guide me on my decisions about the next arrow.

5 Loose Ends

I make no apologies for the title of this chapter. The pun has serious undertones. We loose the bowstring and we shoot in ends. Some ends are shot too loose and do not produce tight groups. Our thinking can be so woolly and undisciplined that our minds arrive at a loose end. What I do apologise for is putting a collection of aspects of shooting in one loose pile, many of which are vital to good shooting. They may even include your pet subject; certainly one of your personal demons.

But the logic I have used is that the previous chapters have attempted to develop a sequence, or inter-relationship, of the factors making up this frustrating action we call shooting the bow. You will have been aware that many aspects are missing from my discussion of making a shot, but as I said before, there are too many things to think about in any degree of detail, even to the exclusion of sentences. The omissions I made were quite deliberate; they are subjects which need separate study and contemplation to do them, and ourselves, any justice. So to start with my first, apparently gross omission, I want to talk about aiming.

AIMING

Because the bow is a projectile weapon, it is understandable that aiming would surely be put at the top of the list. If you talk to a pistol shooter, or rifleman, it is certainly high on their priorities. But for the archer, aiming, in the sense of sighting the bow, is secondary to the act of releasing the arrow from the bow. The firearm shooter knows that all of the bangs have the same power; the archer's 'bang' can sometimes be a very pathetic affair!

Before you remind me that the peak of concentration for the archer is when the sight is on the mark and the arrow is released, let me state my case. The archer *aims his whole body to make the shot*. The bow-sight gives the archer consistency of aim from one shot to the next; it contributes very little to the consistency of the arrow hits, from one to the next, as any instinctive archer will prove to you. So, if the body is aimed and the bow-sight is for sighting, what are the factors which affect the aim of the shot?

The object of the shot is to release the power of the bow consistently and in line. Successfully holding the bow at full draw is the result of controlled tension within the body, and it is this tension which increases the stability of the archer at full draw. The bow can be sighted much more steadily when fully drawn than when drawn an inch or so.

This means that the whole body is being aimed to keep the sight on the mark. Movement of the sight-pin is movement of the body. To achieve this, the aiming of the shot must start from the stance and the first draw. When the bow is raised to shoulder height, the bow-sight is set against the gold in order to set the body. That is, spine and shoulders are properly aligned with the target, and the sight-pin's position is your visual confirmation of this situation.

The completion of the draw is along this line of aim, even though the sight-pin may float away from the mark. At this stage the emphasis is not maintained on sighting the bow-sight at the centre. Many archers, including myself, will often look at the arrow pile to check the length, to balance the sense of power of the shot against the draw length.

After that, the sighting of the pin on the target becomes your focus of concentration. The bow-sight will move as you build towards release. The fitter you are, and the more relaxed you are, the less that movement becomes. If you see the pin apparently rigid in the centre of the gold, the odds are that you are so tense that you have little chance of making a good release. An observer would see your sight moving across the target face as your whole body moves in space, pivoting round the sight-pin.

I am aware of the sight-pin as something which should be in the centre of the target, especially when I release, so I am continually letting it move into the centre. Not putting it but letting it; and, after many years of shooting, it is one of my habits, one of my good habits. With this concept of aiming in my mind I can measure the relaxation level of my body because the sight-pin seems to 'float' on the better shots and, what I believe is equally important, the sight is moving towards the centre of the gold, more often than not, when I release.

Many years ago, I went through the 'coming down onto the gold' phase, or even the 'panning across' phase, but I ended up continuing the movement as I released. The results were poor. With modern, properly stabilised bows, the reaction of a bow is so predictable and consistent that the fewer non-aligned actions we make, the better.

We are now left with the mechanics and physical design of the bow-sight. I have used the rather specific term 'sight-pin' when referring to the bow-sight, as a simplification merely to be consistent. There are many designs for the sighting element which are available, so a word or two is appropriate. The sole purpose of the sight element is to give the archer a consistent and definable image combining the sight and the target face itself into one picture before the aiming eye. The colours of the outdoor target archery face may be pleasing to the spectator but they are far from ideal as a focal point in all sorts of weather and light conditions. That gold has a strong emotional focus, though!

The three basic sighting elements are the pin, the aperture and the cross, for I refer, of course, to the standard FITA rules and exclude unlimited rules which allow peep sights in the string and prism foresights on the bow. The choice of which element to use is purely personal because they are seen differently by different people, depending on the condition of their vision. A long-sighted person has difficulty in seeing the sight element clearly so he may have preference for an aperture, or a large pin, which will form a blurred but identifiable image against the target face. Conversely, the short-sighted archer never sees more than a blurred target face so a finely detailed element is easier to align. If the aperture elements seem too solid, and cover up too much of the target face, then the broken cross gives you the image of an aperture with a blurred disc surrounding it.

The object of the bow-sight is to produce a clearly *defined* image. It is not a clearly *focused* image. That is almost impossible without the use of a microhole lens immediately in front of the aiming eye to increase depth of field in the same way that a camera iris diaphragm operates. When I am tired, or the light is poor, I focus on the sight element and see it against a blurred target face.

An anecdote comes to mind. When I first became acquainted with the PAA Indoor Round with its plain white centre on a completely black background, I had a most startling experience. The bow-sight I had been using outdoors had a large beaded pin as the sight element and I had not used it at twenty yards on the PAA face. When the sight-pin aligned exactly on the centre, the white aiming spot disappeared behind the pin; everything went black!

The extension at which the sight-pin is mounted can vary considerably, as can the engineering of the whole bow-sight assembly. It needs only simple geometry to demonstrate that the longer the distance between the eye and the sight-pin, the more precise can be the aim. The big problem for us archers is that muscle vibrations are amplified for the same reason. So use the long extension with caution.

Bow-sights can be very expensive and beautifully engineered, but be aware that you are paying for what you get, not necessarily what you want. All you need is something to line up with the centre of the target and which you can adjust left and right, up and down, for windage and range.

CONCENTRATION

This is not going to be some deep technical or philosophical presentation of the modern concepts of sports psychology. It is, I hope, the thoughts and conclusions which have helped me to understand the problems of trying to carry out consistently, and in a controlled way, the mechanical action of shooting an arrow out of a bow.

The word concentration is, in itself, misleading

The bow sight confirms that the archer's whole body and his tackle are correctly aligned.

because we have used it, and had it used upon us, in such emotional ways that it really means anything you like to make of it. Yet we still use the word. At school we are told to concentrate on any activity which failed to reach the teacher's standard. And in sport we are told to concentrate on what we are doing or, more accurately, on what we should be doing.

Being, as I am, qualified in chemistry, my training must have helped me to form physical analogies for such abstract thoughts as concentration, and I started with a simplistic definition that concentration meant putting aside the unwanted items. This was to get me away from the schoolday concept of cramming the object of focus into an already full brain.

The important word which I use repeatedly is *awareness*. Previously, I have used it in the sense of understanding yourself, but now it can be used in its ultimate sense of *concentration*. The two words are each developing the other in an endless circuit, driven by your own motivation; your ultimate singleness of purpose. We have seen in the earlier chapters what we are aware of. We are aware of what we are *doing* not what we are *trying* to do.

If we set a goal such as a certain score for the round, or to beat some particular opponent's score, then awareness of this goal becomes a barrier to the clear path of achievement. And we feel the emotion of anxiety. Fritz Perls, the founder of Gestalt therapy,

AIM AND CONCENTRATION
1. *Predraw establishes the baseline of aiming. By this stage the archer should concentrate purely on the here and now.*

2. Line develops and concentration is maintained.

states that "anxiety is the gap between now and then. If you are in the now, you cannot be anxious because the excitement flows immediately into the outgoing spontaneous activity".

Concentration is being in the here and now. Your awareness of the whole of yourself puts aside anything which is not relevant to the here and now. For us archers, the shot already in the target is not part of the here, likewise the final score for the day is not part of the now. These are the extremes of our spectrum of thought and are hence the earliest entities which our concentration puts to one side. It takes but little imagination to put aside thoughts of the score for this end of arrows; to put aside the score for this arrow, leaving us the awareness of making the shot which we are making *now*.

The result of a shot must not feed back into the conscious, decision-making mind until *after* the arrow hits the target. Now our concentration centres on the group itself. As a result, the odds of the other arrows in that end also hitting the same target area are greatly increased. When you are shooting well, and feeling on top form, it is possible to build an almost impregnable cocoon of concentration. It is a very good feeling.

The concept of concentration being the 'here and now' includes within itself the concept of not *trying* to make the shot, but simply *doing it*. There is no concern for success or failure; these two are products of setting a goal for the shot. There is just the awareness of doing the whole thing in the way which you set out to do it, in the way which you planned to do it.

There is no anxiety about planning to do something because it is in itself creative; anxiety comes from judging the degree of success or failure. With total

3. Anchoring and alignment of the sight pin with the target completes the sequence. The entire archer/equipment/technique package is now fully concentrated and aimed at the target.

awareness you can pinpoint that part of the whole shot which was not carried out as you had planned it. The position of the hit will confirm the degree of deviation and you become ready to fulfil the whole shot more skilfully the next time.

We cannot achieve perfection since it does not exist. We have to learn to live with the *seeking* for perfection. To have the right mental attitude on the day of our tournament is not enough. You need to be a person who has a fresh outlook on life itself. Our performance is the reaction which we make to the environment, the wind, the sun, the rain, the field. The concept of awareness developing from, and into, concentration is not an abstraction that is difficult to formulate into the real world. It can be demonstrated to yourself in a practical way.

If you become aware that you are not standing as straight and tall as you want to, then you will automatically start to straighten your spine. Awareness itself alters that which is being observed. You will not think of the vertebrae of your spine or the particular muscles of your back; you will simply think of 'tall' and be aware of what, to you, 'tall' is.

It becomes easy to translate this into the simpler requirements of your shooting technique. If you are aware of the bowstring touching your chin, then you can increase the pressure to the firmness which you desire by thinking about it. Your knowledge of how to shoot means that the bodily action will be from the movement of the drawing elbow, more into line with the arrow, but you will be *aware* of the pressure of the string against your chin.

Your concentration, as I have now defined it, will allow you to control the finer details of shooting so long as you have learned the requirements of technique. It is this transient lack of interest in the result of a shot that characterises the champion archer – an abandonment of yourself in the total effort of being as one with bow, arrow and target.

RELAXATION

This is the third of my trio of essentials of the art of shooting which needs separate discussion away from that intensity of the mind when making a shot. Yet the physical relaxation of the body, which is what we seek, is partly impeded by our mental intensity. We need to stand back and look at the problem and make some simple definitions.

Relaxation is synonymous with concentration; they both involve the elimination of the unwanted aspects of the whole body (and mind) at a particular moment. The physical balance of the body (in the sense of muscles and bones) equates with the psychological balance of the mind.

When we talk about bodily relaxation in the context of the extreme muscular tension required in archery, the difficulty is of understanding how you can relax muscles when a supreme effort is expended on holding the rapidly increasing drawing load of the bow, holding the sight still, and on trying to stay upright. So

4. Concentration and aim are maintained well into the follow through.

often when an archer is told to relax, he can only collapse.

What we are seeking is muscle control – individual muscle control almost to the physiculturalist's muscle-isolation. Stated like that, it seems out of the reach of the average weekend archer. Not so; we are back to knowledge and understanding, and to learning how to reproduce a feeling, or sensation, which means that our body is functioning the way we want it to.

At full draw, as the weight of the bow on the drawing fingers feels heavier and heavier, and the sight is in the centre of the target, relaxation means *not tensing* those muscles of the shoulders and arms which are not needed to hold the draw length. It means letting that small movement extending the draw length happen without hindrance.

In our normal, everyday lives, we seldom use our muscles beyond a third or a half of their maximum capacity, so we have no need to use them efficiently or selectively. Our first task then, is to develop our awareness of the bodily functions over which we have a conscious control, not just for archery but for the whole body. There are two basic relaxation techniques:

1. Active – which involves the tensing of muscle groups in order to induce relaxation.
2. Passive – which requires mental concentration on the whole of the body functions and on the parts of the body. Yoga Nidra is an example of this form of practice.

Both techniques require the subject to be lying on his back, and are best learned from a tape-player. Beyond that, the two are fundamentally different. The active technique requires that you tense the muscles systematically throughout the whole body by actual movement and holding the tension, and the breath, for several seconds before relaxing the effort. Like all relaxation techniques, the method and intensity of breathing play a vital role in forming the basic rhythm of the exercise. What is learned by this technique is the feeling of a relaxed muscle as being the opposite to the feeling of a muscle in tension or even in spasm. You learn relaxation as being the state you are not in when you are tense.

The passive technique requires no movement at all. Movement is actually forbidden. The mind concentrates first upon the bodily functions (heart, blood, digestion, senses, and so on) then develops to include the whole body. Your thoughts then systematically dwell on each part of the body (fingers, wrists, arms, and so on) and end with total awareness of the whole.

Both techniques finish with the introduction of induced sensations on the calm body – feelings of hotness or coldness; feelings of lightness or heaviness; and controlled illusions of being in some other place which we can individually associate with calmness, peace and contentment.

There is a place for both techniques in developing the requirements of relaxation in archery. The active approach may appeal more to the Western mind, being not so mystic as the Eastern contemplative approach.

Chest muscle tension prevents the arrow coming through the clicker.

Relaxation is essential to good shooting. Remember, you are not at war with the target.

It does give a positive demonstration, which is self-induced, of what a relaxed muscle feels like, even if the muscles which you wish to relax are not the ones which you learn to relax initially. The passive approach is considered by many sportsmen to be the ultimate in relaxation attainment but, I repeat, both techniques have a lot to offer. For myself the active method can give a rapid response after shooting because the act of shooting involves the body being in a state of static tension. We need to unwind more than a sprinter does. But the passive technique gives the greatest long-term benefit since it can be used anywhere and at any time. With practice it becomes possible to induce a state of relaxation simply by thinking about it whenever the feeling of tension invades the act of shooting.

The immediate result of using relaxation methods is the development of an ability to induce relaxation in separate muscle groups, at will. The connection with the archer at full draw is immediately apparent. When I talk about relaxing the forearms in the hold position ready to loose the arrow, I must know how to relax muscles at will, and this must be learned separately from the act of shooting.

If you practise tensing and relaxing the forearm without relaxing the wrist of the bow hand, then the *thought* of relaxation, as in the passive method, will let the muscles relax. The exercise can be carried out when standing next to a vertical pole, the hand pressing against it, without gripping, with the arm at shoulder height and bent. Flexing and relaxing the muscles of the wrist, forearm and upper arm can be carried out until you can identify the particular group by sensation alone.

The drawing arm can be treated in a similar way, but this time it can be done as a simple isometric exercise. If the two hands are hooked by the fingers in front of the chest, with the arms at shoulder height, tension can be applied to give a small pull of one hand against the other. As before, the muscles of the forearms can be flexed and relaxed at will.

If the fingers of the 'hook' are relaxed as in the action of loosing the string, the arms will fly apart several inches. When the forearms only are relaxed, the drawing arm will stay level but the hand will flop down, hanging loosely from the wrist. Still retaining the hands hooked in front of the chest position, try another archery-related exercise which improves control of tension in the shoulder girdle. Hook the hands together and apply a fair degree of power into trying to pull the fingers apart. Then start to breathe evenly and slowly, in and out, without losing any of the pulling power of the arms. After a few trials you will find that you can do the exercise without tremors or movement of the elbows. This exercise develops the feeling of back tension without any reciprocal tension in the chest muscles. *It is tension in the chest muscles that stops you drawing the arrow that extra fraction of an inch through the clicker.*

One of the invidious aspects of muscle tension is that it increases the more we get tired, so when you start a day's shooting you are more relaxed than after you have shot several dozen arrows. This is due to the body's compensation systems whereby an overworked muscle is protected, by adjacent or even opposing muscles, from permanent damage. When archery is correctly practised there is minimal chance of damage, but our bodies heed the warning signs and this gives us the wrong muscle state for shooting.

Exercises which are designed to increase strength can merely increase tension in the muscles which in turn reduces the smoothness required for archery. What is essential to the archer is muscle *control*. Relaxation techniques increase our awareness of our muscle condition.

One final point about relaxation or concentration concerns peace of mind. Nobody shot a winning score after a row with his or her spouse, or a battle with the kids. It is your way of life that makes relaxation easier. Aggressive sportsmen seldom last long and archery is a stamina sport. The aggression we see everywhere and in other sports is a barrier to good performance in archery. In seeking that self-discipline so essential to a good shooter we seek a calmness, and the path to that starts with relaxation.

6 Tournament Tactics

Archery is a competitive activity. We shoot to hit the mark; and once you start counting the hits you are either competing against yourself or the number of hits you made the last time you shot, or you are comparing your score against the leader board. A tournament is the formalisation of this rivalry and can be set in the sylvan splendour of a field archery course, on the expanse of close-cropped grass of a target meeting, or in the noisy stillness of an indoor range. Your first experience of a tournament will most probably be in the confines of an archery club, amongst friends.

The common factor of all of these places and times, no matter how far from home, is yourself. You as a person, you and your equipment, and you and your technique; all of these you take wherever you shoot. At a tournament you find out just how good they are, and how skilful you are with that beautiful bow of yours.

Tournaments are also times of forgetfulness; forgetting to bring some part of your equipment, forgetting your bad weather clothes and, what is most painful of all, forgetting how to shoot! It is now when you start to be aware of, and fully understand, the need for a discipline in your shooting and self-discipline in your whole approach to the sport. You must develop habits that generate the required discipline.

When you participate in a tournament, the preparations are always the same, starting from your first arrival at the venue to shooting the first arrow. Following the same routine every time will avoid those sudden stomach churning panics when you find something missing or not enough time to be completely ready. These kinds of routines are close to being rituals but they must never enter the category of superstitions. The habits you train yourself into are the cockpit drill of the pilot, because like him you are ultimately responsible for your own fate. The old saying that 'if you haven't brought it with you, you won't find it here' was never truer than in archery. The danger is that even if you have brought it with you, you can still lose it.

TOURNAMENTS AND PRACTICE

Taking up the theme again that the common factor in all of your shooting is you the archer, it is important that you establish the right relationship between the shooting which you do in practice and that which you do in the tournaments. The actual shooting will be the same but your attitude will be different. The fact that it is a tournament and, therefore, more competitive with regard to your fellow archers, or with your personal scores, will overemphasise the desire to score higher.

Too often your practice groups and scores are of a good standard, yet that standard is lost the moment that you are in the tournament even though you are working hard to achieve the control over the shots. Here lies the source of the problem; working at the shots. The rule to follow is that you *work in practice* and *shoot in tournaments*.

Practice is not a time for shooting with gay abandon to prove your skill to yourself. It is when you work on your technique to find the strengths and weaknesses, a time to over-emphasise some part of your set-up so that you are aware of what causes you to shoot incorrect shots. It is when you learn about your technique and your control. The tournament is when you learn about yourself – the real you!

I cannot just shoot at targets 'shooting for groups'. I need the valuation of the scores to know if I am centring the group of shots. I can see if I have shot a group, but I must score every arrow to make me work in practice. In the tournament this becomes the habit I need: to be constantly correcting my aim and

STEVE HALLARD – British Record Holder, 1300 FITA

Steve Hallard's relaxed, accurate shooting is the result of hours of practice. His automatic form and unwavering concentration pay dividends in major tournaments.

technique, to maximise the points per arrow. It is at the practice butts that we learn the rhythm and discipline which will carry us through the crises and tensions of the tournament.

PEAKS AND PLATEAUS

Your objective at a tournament is to put up a good performance; to put up a good score for the whole of the day, or days. There are two ways of approaching this. The first is to ensure that everything comes together right, on the day, so that you and your equipment are both at their best. The second way is to reach a level of performance at which you will put up a good score on the day, or on the day after that. These two approaches are referred to as peaks and plateaus, respectively.

A *peak* is defined as having a day and a performance to which all training is aimed so that you reach maximum nervous and physical effort on the day. This is not wanted in archery.

A plateau is defined as your being continuously trained to maintain performance at some particular level dependent on:

1. Time.
2. Money.
3. Sacrifice.

The plateau is held regardless of repeated demands to perform, or your emotional state.

When shooting to the concept of plateaus (ie predictable scores) you will become aware of the demands made upon you and how much they affect you. The simple list given above can be developed by each individual. The time you have available for both training and tournaments has to be stated quite honestly to yourself and used to the greatest effect (see my remarks on working at practice). Money is perhaps not a major factor – but be realistic, spending a lot of money travelling to every tournament available could be wasting time you could spend more profitably on constructive practice which raises scores at the selected tournaments you do attend. Spending a lot of money on the latest bows and arrows, or sights or whatever,

may improve your scores. But it can impair your emotional state if they don't improve.

Sacrifice is a rather neat title for how your archery fits in with your life, your work, your home, your spouse, your family. It is too easy to become a fanatic; better to be an enthusiast and still be able to live with people. If you are a professional you still have these same choices and decisions to make but if, as with most of us in archery, there are other aspects to life, decisions have to be a little different.

From a more practical point of view, we can define any plateau as being the scoring band (say, 1150–1180 FITA) that you can reasonably expect to attain as reward for the level of work, time and effort you have put into your shooting. It is little affected by weather.

To rise from one plateau to a higher one will be the result of putting more into your personal equation. This may be some improvement in the physical technique of shooting, or in your general health and fitness. It may be the result of a change in equipment or, more likely, in the tuning of your present equipment. It may be that a reorganisation of your lifestyle allows more time to practise. What will be certain is that you will need to put something in to get something out in the form of higher scores.

This concept of plateaus has a hidden advantage in the reverse way. If you know that you *cannot* put all that is necessary into your shooting, such as time, or health, or money, then you can predict a correspondingly *lower* plateau. This aspect does wonders for your level of confidence. You are not left *hoping* that it will all come back; you know it will when circumstances allow you to put it all together again.

This leads conveniently to my personal definition of *confidence*. It is born of knowledge and experience. If you know how to shoot, and you have done it well before, then you can do it again.

TOURNAMENT ENVIRONMENT

Shooting bows and arrows is very much a battle with the elements, subject to the environment. If you are shooting a tournament at your own club on your own range, you have the comfort of the familiar things and the advantage of local knowledge. When you shoot

Absolute confidence is the result of knowledge and experience. Top archers like Pauline Edwards are not flustered by the wind. They accept the conditions, and concentrate on shooting their arrows.

away from home these factors are missing, which lowers your confidence and raises your level of anxiety.

Since you are so alone on that shooting line, you must be very aware of yourself. It is important to have a clear image. What level of truth you can accept? Can you form a confident image of yourself in the new environment?

This imagery of the venue can be based on memory of a previous visit, or, in the case of a new venue, by research. It is worth the effort of finding out what to expect at the ground, or range, by reading any literature available or asking around for details from those who have been there before. It saves a lot of stress if you have a general knowledge of the layout of the field; whether open or green, the aspect or position of the sun, where the toilets are, how far to walk to your target place.

When I travelled overseas to shoot for Britain, I always read as much as I could about the country in which the Championships were to be held; about the town, about the food, the weather, the history, so that very little surprised me when I got there. It is well to remember that we are all strangers outside our own homes. The sooner that you can revert to your true self (which is you, your equipment, your technique and your level of performance), the sooner you can achieve that ecstatic relationship between you, the arrow, and the target.

At the tournament

Once the big day arrives and you stand on the tournament ground, the tension of the event seems to alter your whole bodily functions, almost to the point of embarrassment. The reactions can range from an increased urgency over bladder and bowel movements, to a restlessness and a tendency to inconsequential chatter. Some archers want to crawl into a hole, into the silence of their own minds, except that there is no silence. The world may seem to be moving too quickly for you; or you do everything with a nervous agility. One thing seems dominant in that you want the action to start because the waiting is playing on your nerves. You almost certainly have 'butterflies' in your stomach!

The first thing to recognise is that this body reaction is quite normal; normal that is to the archer who is trained and eager to perform. What is more important

is the degree of tension which you feel. Tension in this nervous form is essential for good performance *if held at optimum level*. If the level reaches an excessive degree, then control over bodily functions is lost, judgement is impaired, actions become uncoordinated, rigidity appears and ultimately paralysis of some muscles can result. At the other end, with only a minimum of tension, the result is poor muscle tone and sluggish actions when sharpness is required.

Some people need to raise their level of tension to reach the optimum while the others need to use relaxation techniques to reduce the initial peak of tension at the start of the event. Very few can hit the right level naturally. It is a trained response, as I said

The British team in action at the 1984 Diner's Club International match.

earlier in this chapter, based on the routines and disciplines learned at the practice butts.

Nearer the end of the tournament a totally different physical condition appears – fatigue. Although we have all of the symptoms of acute tiredness, the fact is that the sense of fatigue is more mental than muscular. Shooting the bow is not that energetic, or athletic. Most men are using only 45 to 50 per cent of their maximum strength to draw their bow; women, on average, use a higher percentage (up to 70 per cent). The physical effort is spread over a long period, and is carried out at our own speed.

What we really experience is loss of mental control. Concentration slips. We forget details of that repetitive body action called technique. This can often be demonstrated when there is a break in the repetition of shooting, such as a temporary stoppage of the competition. After the delay interest revives and tiredness reduces to a degree beyond normal physiological recovery times. Alternatively, if there is a sudden disturbance to your own shooting, such as a string breaking and having to be changed, the ability to concentrate on the task in hand increases dramatically. There is a physical way of minimising this feeling of fatigue, which brings us back to breathing and stomachs. The inactive stance of the archer at full draw does allow blood to pool in the legs. This can be minimised by a simple exercise on the line. Hold your stomach firm, breathe evenly from the diaphragm, and alternately tense and relax your leg muscles.

Tournaments involve the handling of crises, personal crises which are common to all of us whether we are a high performer at a major championship or a club archer shooting on a club target day. It is the handling of these crises which involves the mind of the archer; and it is more than a question of the archer's technique. Crises in archery are a lonely experience and the answer must come from within. There needs to be a faith, or a belief in oneself, and that only comes from a knowledge of yourself based on an honest, personal appraisal.

SIGHTING SHOTS

One of the first crises you experience occurs rather depressingly before the scoring really starts; when the sighters for the day are shot. We can all recall the scene. You are shooting at an important tournament, the season is well under way and you have been shooting to quite a good standard at the club and at practice, although modesty precludes too much reference to scores. You have had a good journey, the day is fine and clear with only a light breeze, you feel well prepared and quite relaxed. The whistle blows and you shoot your turn on the line. The first three shots feel beautiful, middle all the way, so you don't even need to 'spot' them with the binoculars. You come off the line with a relaxed sense of wondering what happened to all the nerves. The second trip to the line is not quite the same, but still produced three high-scoring arrows. Maybe the fifth was a bit weak and the last took a little too long to get away, but they all hit towards the centre. You sit down and spot the whole six; 10, 9, 8 for the first three, 9, 4 low, and 6 for the second. A 46 end at 90 metres! What do you do now? First you multiply it by two . . . a 92 dozen. Times three is 276 for the first range of a FITA round. That has to mean 300 for the 70 metres so . . . just relax, calm now . . . we are looking at the thin end of a possible 1220 FITA round! When the whistle blows again for the scoring arrows the second thing you consciously do on that day is to wonder 'how do I keep that up?'; and you shoot your next six arrows trying to remember how you shot the sighters.

With the benefit of your years of experience you manage to salvage a panicky, sweaty end to score 32 points, and one arrow off the target. The day has lost its ethereal quality and by the second dozen you are working to some sort of plan. But the third dozen was really rubbish. You settle down to the hard graft that your shooting usually is and you are on the way to a 1000 FITA. Maybe, with the right company on your target, you can regain some confidence to make 1050 points.

'Why is it that when I shoot a good end for sighters the round is sure to be a poor one?' We have all heard this cry from the heart, even if it was only resounding inside our own head. The answer is partly a lack of understanding about your own way of shooting, and partly not using the sighters profitably. The members of this 'sighter-syndrome' group are usually the experienced but mediocre scoring shooters who are more aware of their shooting the more practice they can put in; they soon go off the boil after a break in shooting. It is seldom that novices have sighter arrow problems and the top archers certainly do not.

So, if you practise regularly, set up your tackle well, impose self-discipline and dedicate yourself to self-improvement, you still lose out. Why? Because your thinking must be wrong. If you are willing to accept that there are two levels of consciousness (the conscious mind and the unconscious mind), then you have to let the conscious mind trust the unconscious; and to do that you need to understand the part that each plays in your shooting form.

These different levels of mind, or levels of self, have been given many names, but let us call the unconscious mind the *inner mind*. It is the level of consciousness which learns to do things; it is the one which we train when we practise shooting; it is the creature of habit.

The *conscious mind* is the one which directs, chooses, decides and judges. It is the mind which plans the practice wherein the inner mind learns its habits. So, what has this to do with those sighter arrows? Quite a lot. With plenty of practice behind you and a general feeling of contentment and ease, the first arrows were shot by the inner mind, out of habit, out of good habits. While they were being shot the conscious mind had no controlling awareness about the actions involved in making those shots, so, (and here is the first mistake) the conscious mind, not trusting the inner mind, tried to take over control. Result, disaster. The conscious mind has the difficult job to do, it has to be *aware* of what you are doing without trying to *make* things happen. The inner mind makes things happen – *out of habit*.

The problem about not shooting perfectly all of the time is that we must, by the very nature of things, have practised a lot of bad habits as well. The inner mind, the computer of the brain, doesn't know the difference. It is our conscious mind which has to reject the bad habits and replace the thoughts with the good habits. This is the important concept: your conscious mind must think of the good habits. However, it must not take over and *instruct* each part of the body.

Those first few arrows of the day were shot, as they should be, as a continuation of your last practice session. Your technique ran on 'automatic pilot'; the conscious mind was elsewhere. It was not aware of how you shot, it did not take notes. It did not check on what you were doing. And it did not interfere.

Your own mental computer had put in the right archery tape, the one with the good habits. Then it switched a track and tried one of those easy, bad habits. Your conscious mind should have been aware and put in the right signal . . . a picture . . . a feeling. But it did not.

So much for the psycho-synthesis. What should you have done with those six 'free' arrows which we call sighters? Let us make a list of what you need them for:

1. Windage.
2. Range.
3. Warming up your muscles.
4. Settling in the bowstring.
5. Establishing your 'form'.
6. Identifying today's weaknesses in form.
7. Establishing the concept of 'groups'.

Windage and range are obvious. If you don't find the centre quickly you will lack confidence and use the next couple of ends searching for both the centre and confidence. But how about establishing form at the same time?

Since your conscious mind is very much involved then it is best to have a plan. One which I have used effectively is this. Set your sight to the best of your experience and then shoot a good shot, without aiming too fiercely, but do be aware of where the sight was when the arrow left. If you feel it as a well-shot arrow you will feel some confidence towards altering your sight without wanting a group of four in the same spot. If the shot feels out of line or not sharp enough, and it is on the target, shoot another one before altering your sight. If it goes the way you expected you feel even more confident.

When you alter your sight, make a definite adjustment and then shoot confidently at the new mark. An old trick is to make only half the required adjustment. If the arrow hits four colours out, alter your sight for two colours. There is a degree of sense to this. Your inner mind makes corrections to form as well, and most of us don't shoot nine inch groups at 90 metres.

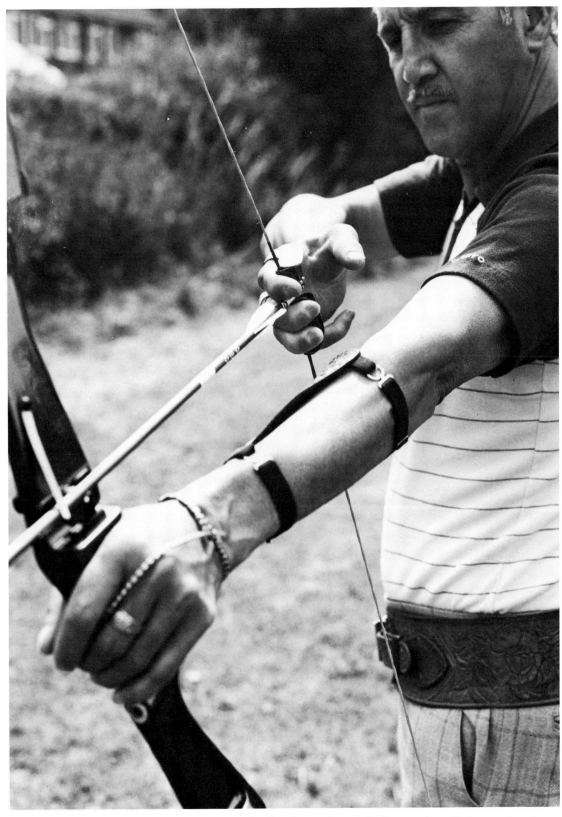

Learn to shoot your arrows from habit. Disaster results when the conscious mind takes over. Once Roy's arrow is nocked, the rest of the shot runs under subconscious control.

Idyllic surroundings and perfect shooting weather.

If, after this adjustment, the arrow hits still two colours out then you know you were right; if it hits centre you are on form. But if you over-correct, down goes the old confidence level. To assess your form, shoot one arrow 'relaxed' and shoot one 'hard', the results will give you a quicker feedback of today's ability to control your form.

The settling in of bow and string is a more subtle aspect of your shooting which you should have evaluated at practice sessions. When you are ready to shoot at a practice session, preferably on a calm day, shoot six arrows at exactly the same mark without changing your sight setting. At the target, note exactly where each arrow hit in the sequence in which you shot them. Record the hits in the form of the clock designation, that is seven at four o'clock, five at eleven o'clock.

After several sessions of recording the first arrows you will be able to see if there is any pattern to the settling-in shots. If there is, such as the first arrow always hits high, or left, or wherever, then this behaviour must be built-in to your sighter routine. Another confidence builder.

SHOOTING IN THE WIND

Probably the next major crisis which we all experience when shooting outdoors is trying to cope with the effect of the wind on the arrow flight. Few archery books discuss shooting in the wind in any detail. Most coaches go no further than the need to aim off in a wind, a point which is patently obvious to the archer standing on the line on a normal shooting day.

Remember that *wind is normal*. We would have a deadly climate without it. One thing is clear to me; you cannot learn how to shoot in the wind like learning to draw the bow – you experience the wind and react to it.

I have been shooting for many years and I have shot in a lot of bad weather. The oldest memories are of frustration and ineffectualness over what to do about the wind. I would be shooting in a championship, trying to decipher a pattern of orderliness out of the random flight of my shafts. Between ends I would listen to the confident assessments of my companions as they read the wind. Then I would start a new end with no apparent progress from the last, just working at it and grafting. Yet at the end of the day, with no satisfaction over the score, I very often collected the gold medal. So, where did I aim?

It wasn't the aiming I remember so much as the feeling of confidence and strength which developed during the day and the changing ranges. Not confidence in my ability to hit the middle but in my ability to make a strong, controlled, in-line shot. That expression 'reading the wind' is so beautiful and so descriptive. You can hear the wind but you cannot see it. What you see is the effect of the wind on the clouds, the trees, the flags, the grass . . . you see it and you read it. Anyone who has stood downwind of me, with a face full of grass cuttings, knows only too well what I mean.

Let us start somewhere and try to build up a picture of what shooting in the wind is all about. Firstly, how do you aim? Do you alter the sight-pin or do you alter the point of aim? The answer is both.

Shooting in a wind shows two components; the drift, which is the average of the deflection from the calm weather arrow flight; and the gusts, those peaks in wind velocity. The aim should accommodate both these components by setting the sight-pin for the drift and altering the point of aim to counteract the gusts. Both settings will change throughout the round being shot, the drift being the more constant and less noticeable at the short ranges. The drift is not felt by you the archer because you are in the moving air all of the time; it is the gusts which you are aware of and it is the gusts which affect the archer more than the arrow. There are times when the wind seems to drop and you are tempted to aim back in the middle, but when the shot floats into the black, you realise that the wind was

completely steady but still there.

So much for aiming. The next question is how to shoot. Should your technique be changed to accommodate the wind? In my experience, the answer is definitely not. What does alter is the time in which you make each shot. In general, it pays to get rid of the arrow fairly quickly instead of dwelling on the aim.

Most archers are convinced that groups inevitably grow wider when shot in the wind. That is not necessarily so. Groups shot by the top performers stay the same size, but lose the odd arrow or two. The strays were either aimed wrongly through miscalculation, or were affected by a sudden gust or lull – by some external influence that pushed them off course at the moment of release.

The only way to keep a tight group is to make strong, well-controlled, shots, and no more so is this required than when you shoot in a wind. Before developing this point let us consider for a moment the different types of winds.

Living as we do in a predominantly two-dimensional world of side-to-side, and front-to-back, we think mainly of the wind as if we are standing in the centre of a giant clock face with the target at twelve o'clock. The wind is then a four o'clock wind from the back to the right of us, or a ten o'clock wind from the front to the left of us. Head winds and tail winds, cross-winds and quarter winds. Different winds have different effects on the arrow flight and, so far as I am concerned, the least effect is from a steady tail wind. Some may say that a steady wind from nine o'clock is the easiest to shoot in but, since shooting in-line is a fundamental weakness of the majority of archers, the cross-wind has a bad mental effect and leads to a breakdown of their technique.

What of the arrow flight itself? It is obvious that because a cross-wind makes the arrow drift, you should aim into it to compensate. But did you know that you must also aim *higher* the further out from the gold you hold? The arrow has further to fly, curving as it does away from the target, so it needs more elevation. When you aim off for a strong gust, make a good margin of windage because if you have struggled for an extra two or three seconds to steady on the aim, the shot will probably be a weak one anyway and, if it isn't, a red upwind makes you feel more confident than a 'floating'

Flowing technique and firm control will put your arrows near the middle even in rough conditions. Often the wind affects the archer more than it does the arrow.

blue downwind.

Head winds are to me very tricky, but interesting as well. You have very little drift, or an almost constant one, but the arrows go up or down with the gusts. A flag on your target does not seem to help, since you are looking at the loose end. Look at the flags several targets away instead, or a tree at the end of the shooting field. The problem with a head wind is that you have to read the wind before it comes to you because you are shooting into it.

A head wind is reasonably predictable because whatever happens it will slow the arrow down; but the tail wind, when it gusts, is a very funny animal. If the gust hits the arrow on the rising part of the parabola, it tilts even more steeply; and if it hits the arrow when it is falling towards the target, the tail rises and the arrow hits low. So, a gusting tail wind needs some reading –

arrows may hit high or low, opposite to your expectations.

Having watched arrows for a while, let us look back at the archer. Off-centre hits attributed to the wind can be confused with those caused by bad shooting – weak and low, out of line, and over-stoked high ones. It becomes vitally important, then, to know the difference. You shot the arrow, so you must decide.

The way to do that is to think more about the shot and less about the aiming. An awful lot are going to be aimed in the wrong place no matter how good you are, so concentrate on good shots, strong, in-line, relaxed, with a clean follow through. Let the aim 'float' and make a good shot even if you are off the aim you really wanted. If the shot hits where you aimed it then remember, that is what the game is all about.

To shoot well in a wind you must be able to shoot

well in calm weather. Your calm weather technique must be strong and flowing, free from violent follow throughs and free from complicated ritual techniques as you build up to the shot. In calm weather the shot timings become uncannily constant as your internal clock takes over but, in a wind, you must be prepared to take less time over the shot so that you can take advantage of the first line-and-aim co-ordination signal. There is no time to crank three-quarters of an inch of arrow through an apparently rubber clicker.

How do you use a clicker in the wind? At the risk of being patronising, I must tell you that if you use the clicker properly there is no great problem. It can only be controlled if the shaft is drawn until the clicker is half-way down the pile in the first couple of seconds. The rest of the build-up of the shot must be without any creeping, hence the necessity of shooting strongly. When the eye-sight-mark trigger occurs, the increasing pressure pulls the shaft through the clicker . . . and the gods and your technique control the rest. Any unnecessary tensions left in your upper body, and the wind will turn you like a windmill. Remember, if all this is outside your ability, at least the clicker stops the arrow blowing off the shelf while you struggle with your private demons.

On the subject of equipment there is one aspect of shooting in the wind which I seldom hear referred to, and that is bow-tuning. Not how to tune the bow to the arrows but the effect of good or bad tuning. Since the wind can be moving across the arrow flight, or gusting towards, or with the flight, an arrow which is flirting from side-to-side as the fletchings try to stabilise it is very vulnerable to gusts. As the arrow swings like a great compass needle, its fletchings may be pushed more to one side than the other, and the arrow appears to have a huge drift component to its flight. It is more important to have a clean, straight exit of the arrow from the bow in a wind than on a calm day.

You cannot completely escape the wind unless you shoot indoors, or take up field-shooting and shoot in the woods, so enjoy it! Be aware of everything that is happening to you, concentrate on good shots and less on the aim and, above all, shoot strongly and confidently.

I cannot finish without one anecdote about the wind. The place was Grenoble, France in 1973. The event, the World Championships. The weather was terrible. The first day was abandoned because the rain storm flooded the ground. Nearly 400 yards of duckboards were laid and we shot the whole first FITA round on day two. The wind was nine o'clock, gusting from 30 to 40 mph. A group of weary British men stood talking.

A voice asks, "Where are you aiming your arrows then?"

Me, "Over in the red."

The voice, in loud disbelief, "The red! I'm right off the edge of the target!"

Me, "I mean the red on your target!"

7 Solving Problems

Considered solely on its title, this chapter would certainly be voted as the subject which most archers wish to discuss first; a pity, since we are dedicated to the seeking of perfection. But the reality of life is that things do go wrong. If you are an optimist you will, of course, say that things do not always go right.

Things do not always go right very early on in your archery career but you are dominated by that most misleading of proverbs; practice makes perfect. It does not; but more about that later. Things can certainly go wrong when you have been an archer for a long time, and here I speak solely for myself. I need no confirmation!

With the best will in the world you think you know

POSTURE AND BOW SHOULDER
1. Stand tall, and set the bow shoulder firmly.

2. *The shoulder remains firm as the draw builds up. The bow shoulder blade is the fulcrum for the rear elbow and its shoulder blade.*

3. *The bow shoulder/arm/wrist must remain firm during extension and release.*

how to shoot, so the reason that things go wrong must be due to things which you do not know, or things which you have forgotten. Since this chapter is really concerned with the archer who has got 'stuck', the second case is usually the relevant one.

Let us take *posture* first. Two things can happen. The longer you shoot, the more idle you become. Or, the harder you work, the more exaggerated your posture becomes. In either case you can be unaware of what is happening to you. What I have rather callously called idleness may be your attempt at relaxation. The spine sags into a less than graceful 'S' shape, with the stomach sagging and the shoulders rounded.

There is only one way to shoot consistently and that is by standing tall. If you want to find out how tall you can stand, then stand with your back to a wall, heels against the bottom of it, and try to hold your buttocks, back, shoulders and head against the wall. You will have to hold your stomach in, if nothing else! If you want to see how you stand at full draw then draw your bow facing, and aiming into, a full length mirror (without an arrow if it is not your mirror!) Look at the shape of your spine and the firmness of your stomach.

Your spine is controlled by the position in which you place your head and, as F. M. Alexander taught in his book *The Use of Self*, the head should be balanced on an erect spine and neck. What becomes obvious as a tournament progresses is the lack of stomach tension when making a shot. If someone asked me what was the minimal exercise an archer needed to do, I would say without hesitation stomach muscle exercises. Most posture defects can be corrected by holding the head as high as possible and holding the stomach firm.

A second aspect of posture weakness concerns the bow shoulder. As beginners we were all taught to hold the bow shoulder back, away from the string path. The reason was painfully obvious when the string hit the elbow and raised a yellow-brown bruise! As our career spans the years we still retain the partial memory of keeping the shoulder back, even though now it is several inches away from the string path. What is lost is the fundamental alignment of the stance. With the front shoulder so far out of line, the act of holding a length becomes difficult because the load of the bow has been transferred more onto the arms, and the release of the string does not produce a smooth follow through.

The answer is to check bow shoulder position at the start of the draw. I like to visualise the drawing thumb extended in towards the bow shoulder as a gauge. The feeling you experience is of getting the shoulders behind the bow. You will shoot more powerfully that way. A bow shoulder that lifts (that is, raised by the pressure of the bow) has little effect as long as it remains in line. Draw length, however, is reduced.

A third aspect of posture is leaning away from the vertical. Although the tendency to lean back over the rear hip is more prevalent since the physical weight of bows increased dramatically with the use of stabilisers, it has been in evidence as far back as the 1800s.

This posture can be simply the result of tiredness developing as the tournament progresses, or it can be the result of exaggeration. At some period in the development of a technique there could have been a feeling of more weight on the rear foot as a better length was achieved. As time passes there remains only the memory of this feeling of a rearward balance and the body reaches ever further, little by little, to maintain it.

Here we see the trap which our senses lead us into, and it applies to many other aspects of the complete posture. If we use only the sense of feeling from the muscles of our body to control the use of the body then we will eventually be misled. Once a particular muscle action becomes a habit we are no longer aware of the effort to repeat that action, so we increase the action to stimulate the feeling – which alters the posture more than we originally intended. This process is quite subtle and unnoticed. As an example, when a child learns to walk it finds, eventually, that it has to lean forward to the point of over-balancing before it can use its feet to make progress. Yet, as accomplished walkers we do not consciously think of leaning forward to walk. We merely start walking, and we automatically avoid a fall.

The answer here is to develop an awareness of posture relative to the position of the bones of the skeleton and not to rely on the muscles of the body. Have someone watch you shooting. Use photographs taken from both rear and side views to see how you do stand, preferably when you have been shooting a while and you are tired. A comparison between photographs taken some months or years apart makes an interesting study. I have a series of three which my wife took of me over three days, prior to my competing in the European Championships. They show how I worked to regain a balanced, upright stance.

SORE FINGERS

It is so frustrating to know that, although you are strong, fit and determined, your fingers still let you down. But do they? Can soreness be the result of what you are doing wrong? Let us start with simple causes, and work our way up.

Just shooting a lot of arrows and shooting in hot, humid weather will make your fingers sore. But the type of shooting tab which you use can have considerable effect on the fingers beneath. If the tab is made of thin leather, you may have a nice sense of feel, but the friction of the string pushing your fingers out of the way may still hurt. For modern composite bows a two-layer shooting tab gives better protection for the fingers and improves the string release. The outer layer which is in contact with the string needs to be smooth and fairly hard, and be capable of folding with the minimum of surface creases. The inner layer, in contact with the skin of the fingers, needs to be softer and give a slight cushioning effect to even out the sharp pressure of the string across the fingers. The main advantage of the two layers is that they can move independently of each other so that much of the string friction is absorbed by the sliding of one layer over the other as the string passes.

My own personal choice has always been for pony butt leather oiled with neat's-foot oil. Putting talcum powder on the surface of the leather has many devotees, but it must be used consistently to avoid varying effects, and it is not much use in the rain.

Still on the design of shooting tabs, a tab which is too small can soon produce sore fingers. If it is too short and does not reach to the end of the fingers, the string passing over the ends of the tab makes the edge of the leather dig into the pads on the finger ends. Similarly, if the tab is not deep enough to wrap round the lower edge of the third finger, then the string can force the edge of the leather into the skin of the finger. This effect is produced during the holding of the bow at full draw, not from the release; and both problems become more pronounced the more arrows you shoot.

The real culprit of sore fingers is the way in which you release the string. It is important to realise that the string *pushes* the fingers away once they begin to relax. You cannot move your fingers faster than the string. The secret lies in relaxation.

What you should not do is fling the fingers open at the release; a moment's thought will show you why. To extend the fingers as straight as possible requires considerable muscular activity in the hand and, since the string starts to move at the same time as you start to extend the fingers, the string is hitting the tense finger ends as it rapidly accelerates.

When you relax the drawing forearm and see, in your mind, the release as the link between holding ready to loose and the follow through after the loose, then the drawing fingers simply relax as they no longer are required to hold the string.

The sensation which I have, as I release, is not that my fingers straighten out; they still feel bent as in the curl of the hand at rest. This can be seen on high speed photography. For the really smooth releases I have a sensation of the hand closing, not opening, into a relaxed but powerful follow through.

Another aspect of the drawing fingers which will not suffer from discussion, concerns the use of each individual finger and how it shares the load of the string. If you look at your drawing hand, palm up and fingers straight with the hand in line with the forearm, you can see that an imaginary line through the forearm is in line with, and divided by, the second and third fingers. Also, the fingers vary in length.

When the ends of the fingers are curled over into a hook, the creases of the first joints do not form a straight line unless the fingers are bent to different degrees. The degree of bend, under the pressure of the string, puts an excessive load on the third finger, which is not called upon to work so hard in normal everyday tasks.

Look back at the hand, palm up, fingers curled. Then twist the hand by raising your thumb. You can see how the first finger is brought more into line, where it can share more of the load. This, I believe,

THE PERFECT RELEASE

The correct, relaxed release does not depend on the archer deliberately opening his fingers. As Roy demonstrates in this high-speed analysis, the STRING pushes his FINGERS out of the way. Because they are relaxed, his fingers actually close after the string escapes.

1

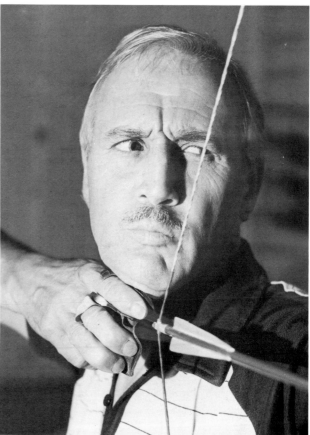

4

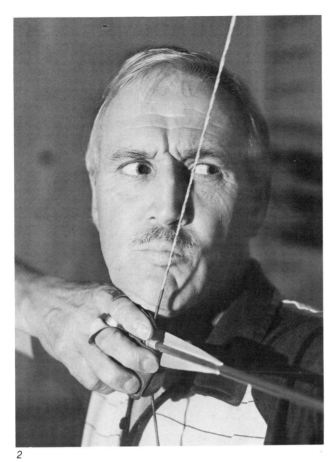

2

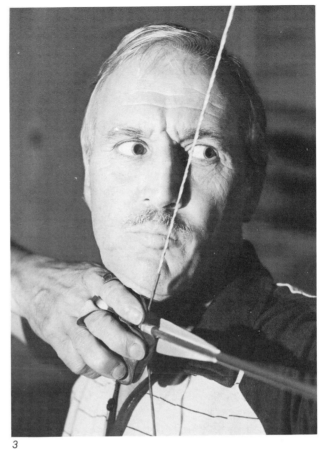

3

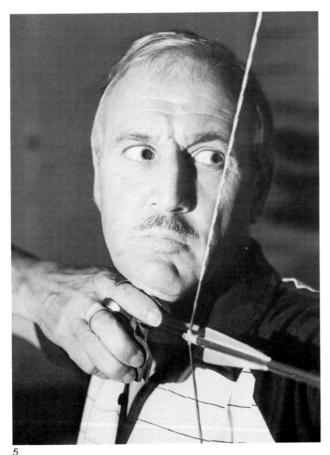

5

6

POWER AND LINE DEMONSTRATED BY STEVE HALLARD
1. Preparing the shot.

explains the rotating action felt in the drawing hand at the final stages of holding the bow. What can go wrong, as your shooting progresses, is to develop a lock that rotates in the opposite direction, and puts more of the third finger and less of the first finger on the string. This can result in dispensing with the first finger entirely and in using the second and third fingers only to hold the full weight of the bow. I do not reject this as a technique. It is used successfully by several very good archers, but must, like any other aspect of shooting, be carefully worked out and justified.

STRING PICTURE

When we talked about aiming, the emphasis was on the image of the bow and the bow-sight against the background of the target. When we are shooting well this becomes the final focus of our concentration. The whereabouts of the string takes a secondary place in this visual stimulus to our minds. There are two reasons for this lack of emphasis on the string image, or string picture as it is often called. Firstly, it is usually very blurred because of the nearness of the string to the aiming eye, although very short-sighted archers quite often can see the fibres of the string material. Secondly, if the concept of sighting with the body, which I have already described, is understood and carried out correctly, the placing of the head will automatically line up the image of the string relative to the bow-sight.

However, when things are going wrong and the weight of the bow is being held on the arms instead of across the back, you can suddenly be aware of a fat, blurred string which seems in the way and you do not know where to put it. Because of the combination of the arms and shoulders being out of the 'line' of the shot and the tense neck muscles twisting the head at too great an angle, the string can appear to be to the left or the right of the bow handle. The string image should be seen just to the side of the sight-pin, between the pin and the bow handle.

The string picture is a secondary check of the head's position when aiming and, I must emphasise, is the result of setting the shoulders and arms in the 'line' of the shot. When you suddenly find that you are very much aware of where the string lies in your aiming picture, you probably have problems with posture and line, as I have described in earlier chapters.

PUSHING AND PULLING

Within the concept of power and line in the shot one can imagine two extremes.

1. A strong bow-arm extended fully with the drawing arm pulling firmly against it until the clicker signals the full length of the draw.
2. The drawing shoulder well back, taking the full load of the bow and the bow-arm pushing to give extension to the final draw length.

Needless to say, there are shooters who use either of these extremes to good effect, but you need to be

2. *Line and power begin to develop during the first few inches of draw.*

physically strong to shoot consistently that way.

Rather than discuss the merits of either pushing or pulling for a moment, let me stay with the theme of things going wrong. If your arrows hit left and right of the centre, but at the right height, then you have lost the balance between pushing and pulling. You have not lost the power; you have lost control of the *line* of the shot.

For a right-handed archer, arrows that hit left of centre are the result of the drawing arm being the weaker. Arrows that hit to the right are due to the front arm being weaker. (If you are left-handed, reverse the process.)

Remembering this simple rule helps you to under-stand what is going wrong with the balance of the power in the shot, and it also makes the question of pushing or pulling much clearer.

For the greatest number of archers, the main weakness is not keeping the load of the bow on their shoulders. When you start the day fit and strong you can confidently pivot the drawing elbow and shoulder on the front shoulder and hold a length with ease. Then the balance of the shot seems even. You can push through the clicker or pull through without losing your line. When tiring or, more likely, having difficulty holding the correct aim because of the wind, you tend to become more rigid with the front arm in order to aim. All the power must be carried on the

3. Full draw completes the development of line and puts the full weight of the bow on Steve's back. Note the relaxed draw fingers, high elbow and relaxed but powerful bow arm unit.

4. Steve extends through into follow through. Only when the bow is on your back can you afford to start thinking in terms of pushing and pulling.

drawing arm. Now the problems start in earnest since the hits fly upwind or down for no justifiable reason.

It should become clear that this balance question is controlled from the drawing arm side of the body. *Not until the load of the bow is firmly established on the back, by the rotation of the drawing shoulder blade into line with the front shoulder, can you consider pushing or pulling. Anything else is shooting off your arms.*

MAKING PROGRESS

Talking about the practice of archery leads us to the rather misunderstood and often dismissed expectation of the sport – namely, how should progress be made?

If we take the score for a given round as the measure of one's skill, should you expect a steady increase as more rounds are shot? The answer is no, I'm afraid. Starting as a beginner and scoring, say, 750 for your first ever FITA, you can see a 50 point increase coming along as a natural progression, a reward for your efforts. You will see the scores climb higher – 800, 850, 900, 950. But each 50 point gain is more and more difficult to attain.

What you find hard to believe (or, more accurately, accept) is that you only get out what you are willing to put into your archery. What really goes wrong is that you expect too much.

The way that your scores build up is in the form of steps which vary in height. Some are up, some are down. My old friend Howard Wiseman, author of *Tackle Archery This Way*, describes it as being like a goat alone in his mountain peaks. He can see the one he wishes to reach but he may have to go down to a lower one and jump around before he leaps upwards to the peak he desires.

That is how your scores will progress; in steps, maybe by 50 points, maybe by 100 points, depending on what you have done to achieve them. The rewards will come from working on your technique, your concentration and on your equipment. But, above all, from making less mistakes. If you really want to see an improvement in your scores you will not get it by shooting better tens or better golds. First make every shot hit the target and score, then keep all of the arrows inside the black ring, no whites. When you get to making all of what used to be blues into reds, you are starting to make good scores.

When you train yourself to hold a bow in this manner, the question of balance becomes a question of extension instead. This may be felt as pressure on the bow, or it may be a movement of the drawing elbow. But the effect will be felt in the follow through which is relaxed and in line.

PRACTICE

Let us finish with the maxim practice makes perfect. How many have been misled by this apparent truth? You certainly need to practise a particular physical activity in order to perfect it, but the objective needs to be clearly defined to stand the remotest chance of approaching perfection. Practice means repetition, and repetition means forming habits – good and bad.

Let us assume that you see practice as shooting a lot of arrows, regularly and with the object of shooting them all in the same way with the results judged solely on whether they all hit the same place. You may have a vague concept in your mind that the 'good' arrows will 'feel right'. Where I fail in this approach is that I am convinced that archery is difficult. If it were easy then thousands more people would be doing it without a care in the world. So when I feel myself shooting in an 'easy' way, the results show it to be the 'wrong' way. The good habits need a lot of preparation, both mentally as well as physically. And, carried out successfully, they are far from easy. They are immensely satisfying though.

Shooting a lot of arrows is not the secret road to high scores. When you hit a bad patch, you must first accept the fact that you are shooting badly. Not easy, that one. Then you must try to understand exactly what you are trying to do, preferably under the supervision of an archery coach. By doing so, find what is missing, or forgotten, or which you just did not know. The weaknesses of your technique will then become apparent and when you practise you can work to strengthen the weaknesses and leave the other parts alone.

This way you generate more strengths and reveal other, lesser, weaknesses. Then you start to strengthen them. I never promised that archery would be easy. It usually hurts; but it is this control of yourself that is the ultimate joy.

8 Making a Come-back

Coaching new archers can be rewarding but it is relatively straightforward; if they do not get it right this session, then they will improve the next time. But what of the real archers, those who made it once and now have to live with their own sense of failure? Coming back out of the despair of lost form is but the other side of the coin of progress, but how can such anguish be described with so little sympathy?

Sympathy is the last thing you need, and I speak for myself. I have been in the depths of despair, and having fallen from a higher level than most three times in my archery career, I learned one hard lesson. I had to accept that I was not shooting properly. No matter what scores I used to shoot or what championships I

Start by making a list of what you do, and in which order. Analyse your shooting as honestly as possible.

Rebuild your style on simple foundations. Above all, learn to develop awareness and control.

had won, I was back at the beginning again. But this new beginning no longer had that bliss, that artlessness of those first months, or years, in archery. There was no novelty in the discovery of archery, no vision of endless new horizons, no elation at the sudden clarity about how to improve the shooting of arrows germinated by the chance remark of a fellow archer. What was left of my previous singleness of purpose, my certain knowledge of how to shoot, was a jumble of alternatives with no confidence in whatever choice I made.

It has occurred to me that on the subject of 'coming back' I am talking to an empty room as sad memories fill my mind of those top-class archers for whom the task of putting it all back together again was too great, too humiliating. Maybe these words will be read by one of those colleagues of mine. I hope so; but they are aimed more at the archer whose confidence is now starting to exceed his knowledge of the art of archery.

So, back to this picture of despair and frustration. A typical specimen (me) lacked any degree of patience about making the shot; and I must admit, did not welcome any outside criticism. There was great difficulty in concentrating clearly on the sequence of building up the shot and finally executing it. There was instead a pre-occupation with the release. It grew worse the more I called upon my memory of half-forgotten mannerisms and tricks.

Here we have the root of the problem. When you have been a good shot, a champion even, you must have known how to shoot, and known a lot about shooting itself. But the necessary understanding and sense of values were still lacking.

We all end up with an imaginary box labelled

Archery Technique, which we fill with anything and everything collected during our career. Our box is just full of the useful and the useless, the workable and the defunct; just like a child's toy box.

When we shoot high, consistent scores the box is used to supply those pleasurable little extras which are sure to add that bit of gloss to an already polished performance. Should the structure of our shooting technique start to disintegrate, the box then becomes a confusion of half-understood bits and pieces. It can even become a nightmare, because somewhere in that box is everything which made up the high scoring, consistent you.

The way back starts by accepting that you are a pretty useless shooter; not ignorant about shooting, just not intelligent about it. Then you have got to start to relearn all about shooting in the bow. Start by making a list of all the things which you think you should be doing, or think that you are doing. Read it through several times. Chances are that the list is not even in a true sequence in time – e.g. thinking about how you draw the bow before how you place your fingers on the string.

Then start to list the items in the sequence in which you do perform them. Rewrite each step clearly, with no vague descriptions. The objective is simplicity. Get down to the basics of your technique. Cut out the useless frills. Then start to practise with your head as

When circumstances forced Pauline Edwards to switch to shooting left-handed, she started from the beginning again and clawed her way back to being Britain's leading woman archer.

well as your body. Above all, forget the scores you used to make. Score your arrows by all means, but do not measure your progress by the scores themselves. You are looking for *control* of your technique and you must learn *awareness*. And you will need plenty of both, plus a great deal of being honest with yourself.

Maybe you will never make it back, but I doubt it. It is much more likely that you will come back as a much stronger archer who shoots significantly higher scores than ever before.

When someone's archery reaches a turning point, a crisis that reveals a proper understanding about himself and shows it to be within his grasp, he just wants to go out and shoot arrows. No more talking about it, or even thinking about it. This is the childlikeness of Zen, which Herrigel wrote about in *Zen in the Art of Archery.*

It is the letting go aspect that characterises the Eastern cultural approach, and it really means the submission of yourself to the complete act of shooting the bow. Make no mistake, we are not talking about some dreamlike state. You will be working harder than you have ever done before. The essential difference is that you will reject the Western concept of external goals. Scores become something of a secondary consideration.

9 Winning

Winning is a solitary activity. At the end of a tournament almost everyone shooting will have lost. Almost everybody, that is, except one . . . the Winner. No matter then how good your technique has become, or how hard you have worked, you had one chance to win. You hear your name. You walk forward and they give you the medal. They call you Champion; of your Club, of your Country, of the World. You were the best on the day . . . you have won. The first time you win there is an air of unreality, even though what you had hoped for has become real. You know that you are tired, but it is not a heavy tiredness, not that lifeless exhaustion of losing. You do not know how you should feel; whether to be elated, or whether to let the moment absorb you.

One thing which you will feel is that you can do it again; that you want to do it again. You will be ruled by the emotions, and you will be blissful in your ignorance. On the day when you start as Champion, the game is then a different one entirely. No blissful ignorance is involved now; you are no longer one of the whole group, striving to win. You are starting as the champion and, until the final arrow is shot, you are defending your rank. At the end of that day, when you hear your name and they call you Champion, then Champion you really are because not until then have you learned what winning really means. Winning is not just shooting well: there is a philosophy about winning which lets you become one with the bow and the target, regardless of all external distractions, and which allows you to conquer the fear which lies within us all – the fear of missing the mark, the fear of losing.

Competitiveness has to be innately creative; any tendency to neurotic competitiveness must be avoided as completely negative. This means that you have to teach yourself the technique required to build up a shot which you *know* is going to hit the centre, and you do this in all humility and with a belief in yourself. You will learn that there are no opponents in archery, only fellow competitors who shoot in the same direction as you, not towards you. You cannot design your game to defeat your opponent, as in tennis; you are solitary, but never alone.

There must be a need to win, just trying to win is not enough, and wanting to win is not the same as a need. I need to shoot well. It is the final abandonment of true confidence which allows the shooting of the arrows to become the end in itself; and the result of the competition becomes inevitable. It is almost like a gamble with yourself where there is no winner and no loser. You may be thinking by now that my words have become intense and hard, as I develop my thoughts on winning; but winning has to be intense and it is hard.

APPROACH

Let us consider two contrasting and somewhat extreme approaches which can be taken in our bid to make the highest score in the tournament. You can imagine it as being like the pack of athletes running in a long distance race; if you get slightly in front of the pack, and then run just as fast as anyone who approaches near you, then you cross the line first. You can, on the other hand, look on the tournament as a time-trial and make your effort hard and consistent, and then emerge from your cocoon at the finish to see how you have performed.

The first concept requires you to be so aware of the performance of the other competitors that you can have little left for your own efforts; you are doubling the demands upon yourself. The second concept has that self-centred intensity and self-discipline which produces record scores, but if you become too easily satisfied in that cocoon, you may emerge with less than the winning score. An archery tournament covers such a period of time that it can only be classed as a stamina sport, and must be approached as such. All through the

MARK BLENKARNE – Commonwealth Gold Medallist

Study Mark's technique and you will see all the
key factors discussed in the book: Line, Power,
Relaxation, Control and Rhythm. These plus his
determination and dedication are what makes Mark
a winner.

hours during which the tournament is being shot changes are taking place. The environment is changing as the day progresses, the light, the wind, the rain. You, as an individual, change physically as your body rhythms go through their different cycles, and your mental condition changes as the memories of each arrow shot build themselves into your total experience of the day.

This is what I mean by being aware of, and understanding yourself. Studying your reactions and conditions helps you to predict the different phases which your body, and mind, change into. But what drives you on, what makes you keep going?

Motivation comes ultimately from a belief in yourself, and that need which I referred to previously. When you are striving for your own personal goal (that is, the tournament which matters to you, the big one) there comes a time during the effort when the mind admits the question of: Why? Why am I here? Why am I punishing myself? It may originate from a sense of impending failure, or a minor loss of performance. It may even originate from the monotony of continual good shots which, in itself, can be a prelude to a loss of performance.

No coach can enter the recesses of your mind. The drive must come from within and you have to let the good habits of shooting dominate. The habit of shooting well, the habit of control, the habit of complete awareness of self. You have to shoot good shots while the mood can be assimilated; then you are back to shooting single shots and being in the here-and-now. For the real champions that question, Why am I here?, is dismissed with the unanswerable question: Why not?

This picture which I am trying to build up of the conflicts and decisions and changes of mood which dominate the archer in his bid to win, are an inevitable part of the long drawn-out effort of completing a tournament. What we are considering is the transition from a technique-intensive event, as in training and learning, to an emotion-intensive event as one makes the supreme effort. Let me repeat this point. When making a winning score the *detail* of the shooting technique itself becomes secondary to the *control* of the shooting technique. The sole objective is hitting the ten-ring, and the sensation is one of feeling strong mentally, as well as physically. Winning scores are the result of the emotional state of the archer, on the day.

It is conventional to state that 'good shooting is in the mind'. Too often the comment is made in the form of an excuse, which it probably is. The majority of archers do not really want to listen to this use of concept of mind in the context of their archery; they want to shoot arrows. The reason for this withdrawal from total involvement in the shooting of arrows, both in mind and body, is the confusion they have about the concept of 'mind'. If I use the phrase 'emotional state', then I expect many more archers to understand me because we can understand emotions: love, hate, anger, compassion, sentiment, nostalgia, envy . . . we call them moods and feelings.

When the word 'mind' is used amongst archers, it is perceived as 'thinking', in the sense of reasoning. What we really mean is 'feeling', the whole sensation arising from what we are involved in doing. By now I have, most probably, lost contact with many readers, simply because I am talking about what goes on in their heads. I cannot apologise, but I can understand. This chapter is about winning and, by definition, that will be accomplished by only a small percentage of archers. How many competitors are there in the tournament which you are going to win?

If you are going to win then you are not going to be beaten. If you are not going to be beaten then you are invincible, and you are going to feel invincible; not arrogant, nor over-confident. You know that everything is right with your technique and your equipment and you feel that you can surmount all the problems and exertions you will face. You are not thinking about winning; your emotional approach is of a winning mood and you feel a winning person.

The next step in these developments is to say that the emotional state which you are in is the personality which you have, the Self which is you at that time. It is not my intention to be abstract. I am still talking about shooting arrows. I am trying to give my own concept of all of those conflicts and elations which I know I have been subject to when winning. Let me try to describe the different emotions which I have personally experienced at one of my winning tournaments. On the journey to the venue, with time passing solely as movement, it is the confident me: I feel in a winning mood today. During the preparations and the sighting shots it is the cautious me, somewhat indecisive as to whether the training and setting up of equipment was really suitable; the 'butterflies' have arrived. Embarrassment loosens my tongue. The long range scoring begins and it is the methodical, reasoning me and, as a thinness of inadequacy intrudes, a feeling of weakness hovers near me. As the scoring arrows increase in their own particular arithmetic, so the rational me, with a veil of nostalgia to smooth the hardness, allows the strength of purpose to progress freely.

The scoreboard is not the stimulator of envy, it is the barometer of the day's capability. The scores above me do not breed any hate or greed, they indicate what can be achieved; what must be bettered. The day progresses and tiredness drags at me like a viscous pool and I am challenged by the doubting, imagining me. What if? Why?

There is an air of unreality; time seems irrelevant to my purpose. My mind becomes sharper as my muscles become duller: if I change slightly the muscles used to set up the shot, it still results in the same tired muscles to complete the final act of power. I become the sensitive, perceptive me. There is a simplicity about what I am achieving in the repetition of the shots. No emphasis on any single part of the whole theme. I feel the line in my tired body, I sense the power in my aching limbs. I am aware of the subtlest changes in my actions, my position in space, and the air itself.

The shooting line becomes the real world and the area behind is limbo; waiting in unreality to return to where the full meaning of the day exists. It is the accepting me: no judgements, whether the arrows nearly touch each other, or one has flown wide; just a knowledge, a belief, in whether I am, or am not, following the path which I have mapped in the completeness of the whole shot, from that first fistful of string through to the final jerk of the sight-pin into the centre of the mark.

I can see the whole arena of the archery field and I can see the individual players; from the voyeurism of watching the ladies in their exertions, to an identification with the men in contention with me. The contest ends and I feel a sense of humility after this journey into myself, a sense of pride at being able to be,

There is an air of unreality; time seems irrelevant to my purpose.

for a day, with my peers as we joined each in his own struggle. This journey through my Archery-Emotions, is just that: it is the archery-me as I shoot to win. It is not meant as a generalisation of how an archer should feel, although I suspect that it is typical of many.

What was intended was to show the difference between will and emotion – the thinking and feeling concepts which I talked about earlier. For instance, I can think that I do not intend to be anxious, but I can still feel anxiety. The feeling does not go away just because we think that it should. When I believe that I can win, I feel that I can win. I do not have to think about winning, only about shooting. We are talking about belief in the ability to shoot well. When you realise that it is through a deeper awareness and understanding of yourself that success becomes more and more the result of your endeavours, you have to learn to accept the you which you see, warts and all; the good and the bad, the things which you would rather forget. Then a deeper level of belief becomes accessible to you. The word I use is mystery; not in its more modern use to simply describe the unknown, but the older meaning of something beyond our rational thought.

THE MYSTERY OF ARCHERY

Shooting in the bow to high levels of performance emphasises the solitude of archery and it invokes feelings of an inner calmness, a sense of both peace and strength. This condition of solitude must only be attainable in a few sporting activities, where introspection is combined with stillness.

For many archers there comes the point when contemplation about Self turns into meditation, and the revelations which are experienced lead into thoughts of a very deep philosophical and even religious nature. There is revealed an awareness of the tremendous potential which we each have within us, focused by the intensity of shooting an arrow, which can lead to a deeper meaning about life itself.

In our Western culture, education and social upbringing has led us to see and believe in the physical aspects of life to the exclusion of the spiritual. But in Eastern cultures, there have always been important parallels between sport and religion. The body is accepted as a spiritual path as well as the mind. There is a reluctance, and even embarrassment, in the contemplation of a possible religious perspective to sport. Our Western minds see self-confidence, and self-determination, simply as secular and materialistic achievements.

The occurrence of peak experiences in many sports is now well documented and accepted as a major concept in the behaviour of consistent, high performance sportsmen, but it is not a state which is planned for. It is the result of a complete commitment to concentration and effort. Descriptions of this state, made by sportsmen, contain a common element which speaks of a new, or higher, dimension to the physical and mental condition which they normally experience in the practice of their sport. It is not a great step from this description to contemplate the existence of a greater being higher than us mere mortals, and religion becomes not a refuge, but a meaning to life. In Yoga, restraint and self-discipline are the first steps, followed by correct posture and breathing. Zen starts with the letting go of the material world with awareness of Self as an independent assessment of your state as an individual performer: arriving at the state where you see yourself carrying out the actions.

We, with our pre-occupation with the material world, attempt to rationalise a new, higher state by using more acceptable words such as 'mental rehearsal' and 'imagery' of the shot which we are about to shoot. We talk about 'psyching-up' as if the whole concept can be defined by a phrase meaning anything to anyone.

What is being discussed is a philosophy about our sport which can carry us through *all* of the experiences; the highs, the lows, the elation, the depression, the frustration, the confidence. A belief in yourself, in a spiritual sense, is based on a form of faith. You need a philosophy about your whole life to allow this state to exist in your archery, without arrogance but with humility. Ultimate faith goes beyond philosophy but the path has to start somewhere.

SECTION TWO

John Holden

10 Coming to Terms

Books are written for a hundred different reasons, but I suppose that in the history of publishing, *Archery in Earnest* is surely the first to be sparked off by a disastrous FITA round. Back in 1979, that was. My recollection of those last arrows at 30 metres still hurts. Blacks and whites? Wishful thinking! My problem was to keep them out of the grass. And yet the weekend before I had shot a 1000-plus York. What really troubled me was that whereas the FITA was a struggle from start to finish (and only 900 points to show at the end of it) the York had been so, so easy.

Indeed, the pattern of up-and-down scores characterised my shooting that year. Sometimes it went well, sometimes not. That didn't concern me too much. It was far more frustrating not to know *why* one could slap arrows fairly consistently towards the red or better one day, yet could not avoid a string of blacks, whites and greens at the next tournament. And not once in a tournament had I even approached the standard of shooting that sometimes I achieved in practice.

Obviously there was a fundamental weakness somewhere. But how to find it and effect a cure? I read books, watched other archers, listened to a few coaches. Trouble was, I could find little to relate to. Quite a few of the better archers I met were more than willing to forward suggestions, some of which certainly helped in the short term. As for the coaches, they certainly appeared to have all the answers down pat, but where were their successful students? Nowhere that I could see.

Taking time off from yet one more attempt to clone myself into a Pace or McKinney, I began to look at the problem from another angle. I am reasonably co-ordinated; I do not mind putting in the necessary time to practise; and have gone as far as I can to learn the right techniques of shooting from books and magazines, and from watching and talking to other people. My not achieving the standards I seek must therefore be based on some underlying personal weakness.

Namely, I do not know how to make good consistent shots. And I certainly cannot maintain my performance level from one tournament to the next, nor necessarily throughout a single round.

As a result, when my shots go wild I have no baseline to return to. Once 'it' has deserted me for the day, I am stuck. On the other hand, even when I shoot well there always remains a niggling doubt. What if I lose 'it'? Will the next end be as good as this one? How long will it last? And all the while, deep down, I know the answer: I am not in command because I do not understand the essential factors of technique and control. If anything, not knowing why you shoot *well* is more frustrating than not understanding why you shoot *badly*.

As Roy has said, facing up to your personal inadequacies is a harsh business. Long before that FITA brought me down to earth I already knew, had I been honest with myself, that I had only myself to blame. Like the majority of archers who are stuck, I found it too much of a jolt to the ego to look at it that way. It is much easier to blame bow, weather, or 'nerves'; it is comforting in a perverse way to tell yourself that the top shooters are highly talented and secretive. At least it makes a neat excuse. Excuses are the name of the game so far as most stuck archers are concerned.

Eventually, prompted by that disastrous FITA where I missed completely with five arrows at 30 metres, I came to accept that there was a stark choice to make. Either start afresh, or give up the sport. That same evening I dug out Roy Matthews's address from an old copy of *Toxophilus* magazine and wrote to him. What's more, he answered. Thus began a series of letters back and forth in which I asked all kinds of dumb questions, and Roy patiently explained about the elements of good shooting. As a direct result, 1980 was my best year so far. I learned more from six letters than I had gleaned in five years of hammering away at a

STEVE HALLARD – a champion in action

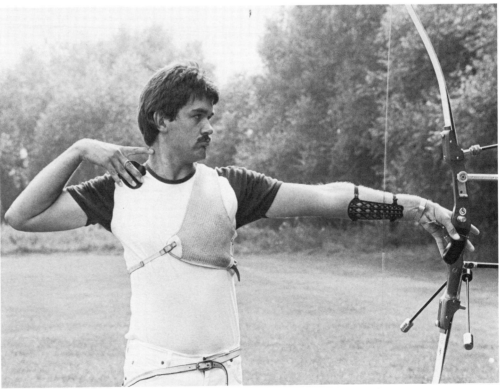

Steve Hallard, first British archer to shoot a 1300 FITA, typifies the power and control found in all world-class competitors. Every top archer has his own unique style, but everyone bases his technique on similar foundations. The main lesson to learn is that there are no secrets. Most archers already know more than enough fact. What they lack is application.

target by myself.

From 1981 to 1983, business took me away from archery and out of the country for long periods. In 1984, I started shooting again on a more regular basis, and not surprisingly found myself very much back to square one. However, using Roy's 'line-power-relaxation' formula, at least I fared better than I would otherwise have done. Then arose the opportunity to add a sports book to my production list. What better than archery? Who better to write it than Roy Matthews? And, from the purely selfish point of view, what better chance to discover more about how to shoot better scores of my own?

There is an important reason why I explain something of the book's background. This chapter did not appear on the original list of topics for inclusion. Instead, it is the result of an intriguing direction that the book seemed to take all by itself. Sometimes it happens this way: a book starts off along a pathway mapped out by author and publisher, then at some stage develops a momentum all of its own. Such is the case with this section. From the archery point of view, the explanation is quite simply that my research into shooting techniques produced results opposite from those I had envisaged.

Like most archers, I assumed that my inability to shoot high scores stemmed from not knowing enough technical information. These days the world seems to depend on facts and figures. In many respects, the more you know, the more competent you become. Yet archery appears to defy that rule; for many frustrated shooters, it is knowing too *much* rather than too *little* that blocks their road to success. More precisely, it is knowing too much about the *wrong things.*

The first two or three chapters of Roy's manuscript fired my enthusiasm and whetted an appetite for things to come. I reckoned, wrongly as it turned out, that his description of basic style and the other foundations to good technique were a prelude to some really juicy bits. In later chapters he would get to the difficult parts, to the secret tactics that must be absorbed and understood if you are ever to be champion. Yet on flipping back through the book, you will find no super-complicated explanations, no secrets, nothing really radical except for the 'line-power-relaxation' formula.

As I worked through the manuscript, I found my whole concept of archery changing. I *looked* for complication and technicality; I *wanted* complication and technicality. So far it's all so . . . well, simple. Hard work, yes. Demanding as well. But surely there has to be more to it?

I resolved to tackle Roy about it when we met for our first photographic session. Pictures first, talk later: that seemed best because then I would have a chance to watch the man shoot. If I watched closely, wouldn't I see some evidence to support my theory that shooting arrows is physically more complicated than he describes? So he shot . . . and he shot. And what impressed me, apart from seeing all those arrows thud into the middle of the target, was the utter simplicity of it all. No fuss, no muttering and head shaking, no sweating to pull an arrow through the clicker. No snatched loose, no deliberately exaggerated follow through.

From first arrow to last, Roy's technique flowed like syrup. Everything he did underlined what he had written about technique. Though his control and mental concentration were obviously rock steady, the physical arms-and-fingers sequence of actions that make up his personal style obviously held no tremendous secrets. On any shooting line in the country you will see dozens of archers doing the same thing, but with one exception. Whereas average clubmen make accurate, controlled shots now and again, Roy Matthews and his peers make them all or most of the time.

The most difficult point for lower-level archers to accept is that the top shooters place more emphasis on *control* than on pure *technique.* Of course, they still spend a great deal of time perfecting the arms-and-fingers side of archery, but the glaring difference between the 1200-plus FITA brigade and the rest is that they have learned to control whatever technique they have. In many respects, the finest archers cannot shoot a gold any better than you or I can. What helps them win medals and shoot for the national team is that they shoot *more* good arrows than we do. As Roy has already outlined, high scores are for the most part not so much the result of shooting more accurate shots as of making fewer mistakes. How do you make fewer mistakes? By increasing your degree of control.

As I watched Roy shoot, my doubts and questions

faded away. It became obvious that there was little that he had not committed to paper already. No doubt he could find more technicality had he wished, but it would serve no useful purpose. To the contrary, by overstressing this aspect of shooting he would have steered his readers towards even greater frustration.

At this point the book changed course to some extent. All along we had intended to feature a number of leading archers besides Roy, to lend variety to the pictures and also to provide some counterpoint to what he had written. Usually there is more than one way to skin a cat; and presumably the archers who agreed to appear would voice strong opinions of their own, some of them contrary to Roy's. In the event, that was not the case. Every archer I talked to – and that includes many besides Mark Blenkarne, Steve Hallard and Pauline Edwards who appear in the book – described archery in his or her own unique way. No two said exactly the same thing. Yet in a sense they all agreed, and therein lies the 'secret' so far as the mechanics of shooting are concerned.

Were time and space freely available, I would have expanded the book to include face to face interviews with a cross-section of leading shooters. But I simply do not have that luxury; and besides, much of it would either be straight repetition or would amount to much the same thing in a slightly different guise. Instead, and to clarify the matter as far as possible, I have taken the notes and tape recordings made during the book's research period, mixed them into one single brew of technique and style, then distilled out the common threads that run through the highest levels of championship archery. What follows is not one person's analysis of style. Rather, it is a composite picture of the key factors that determine how best a modern bow and arrow may be shot. There is no need to elaborate beyond note form, since as you will discover, Roy Matthews has covered precisely the same ground in much greater detail.

Though they may not all use exactly the same description, or indeed exactly the same method of achieving the same result, the majority of 1250-plus FITA scorers base their technique on the following guidelines. In fact, nothing is included on the list unless at least 75 per cent of the archers surveyed counted it as an important factor. If you could grow a test-tube archer and programme him with these common denominators, he would describe his technique something like this.

STANCE

My stance is the result of experiment, and is chosen because it is comfortable and stable. Square and slightly open foot positions suit the majority of archers, but there really are no hard and fast rules. Foot markers? I never use them.

PREPARATION

Preparing for the shot takes place on two planes. Physically, I check the stance, nock the arrow, place my draw fingers on the string and my bow hand onto the handle. Mentally, I run through the whole shot. I actually shoot every arrow twice: once in my head, once for real. Everyone must draw up his own check list. The idea is to be consistent and conscientious.

When I'm happy with the basic set-up, and my mind is absolutely clear about how the shot will build up, I settle my fingers into the string, finalise the bow grip, then pre-load the bow a little by drawing just a few inches. My bow arm and shoulder move partially into position, and I check their accurate placement by feel.

PRELOADING THE BOW

The bow unit – that's the bow itself, my hand, arm and shoulder – swings up into position ready to take the weight of the draw. My drawing unit – string, fingers, forearm and shoulder – also moves into place. By this time, the bow is about half drawn; maybe a little more. The sight lines up with the target, and that takes care of the aim for now. All of this produces a certain feeling, which reflects such things as bow shoulder position, draw fingers and forearm relaxation. If the feeling is right, I proceed. If it is not, either I identify and correct the mistake or I come down and build up the entire sequence again.

DRAWING AND ANCHOR

My priority now is to get everything into line, with the weight of the bow across my back. This is accomplished by physical checks – such as watching the pile draw back under the clicker – but relies more on sensation. The bow arm is important. In fact, it's probably more important to good shooting than any other single aspect of technique. Back tension is another priority, but it's hard to describe. Once you've felt it, you'll know what I'm talking about. Pulling your rear elbow round and well back goes a long way to developing the right tension, and relaxing your forearm helps as well. If you're not pulling with your arm, then you must be using back tension.

And so it goes . . . the draw builds up with that certain feeling, and the string contacts my face to give the right anchor. Right for me, that is. You'll have to discover what works best for you. Exactly what you do probably does not matter too much except for one thing. Getting into line and putting plenty of power into the shot depend on your body being properly aligned so that your back does its full share of the work.

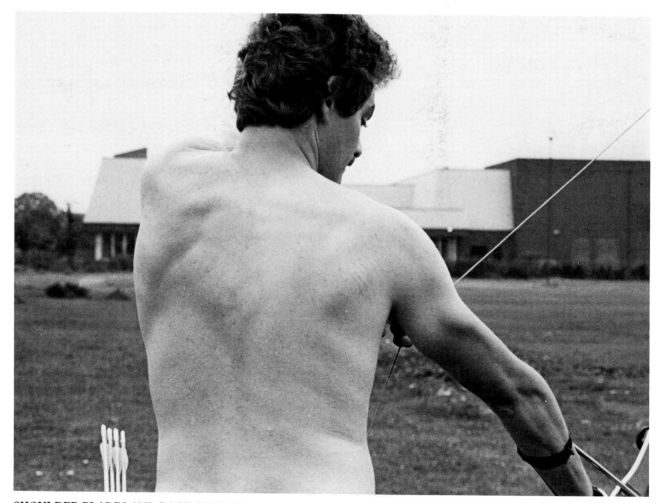

SHOULDER BLADES AND BACK TENSION
Mark Blenkarne's explanation of back tension and shoulder blade action is logical and convincing. By contrast, the traditional advice of 'squeeze your shoulder blades together' clearly misses the whole point.

Sometimes the traditional centre-of-face anchor prevents the rear elbow coming back and around to the correct position. If so, shift to a side anchor. Line and tension are more important than anchoring, and are to some extent even more important than aiming itself.

RELEASE AND FOLLOW THROUGH

Once I'm at full draw and anchored, with that important feeling still building towards its climax, I concentrate on aiming. Then I shoot the arrow and go into follow through. What happens is this. As soon as I'm on aim, I increase the feeling of pressure and extension that already exist due to the way the shot has progressed so far. The arrow pile comes through the clicker, the string leaves my fingers, and because I'm still concentrating on aim and extension, follow through is automatic. I do not force it, though sometimes I think it helps to exaggerate it a little, particularly at the bow arm end. It isn't exactly a push . . . more as if you're pressing the sight-pin into the gold.

Oh yes, you want me to talk about release, don't you? You have to look at it in the right perspective. It is not the final stage in the shot. Good release is something that just happens during that aiming/extension phase. How do you release? Well, basically you just let go. I don't even think about it. If I do, I lose control and tension, the bow comes off my back and on to my fingers. Same applies to the clicker. That click isn't an end point. It's just one more stage in the whole technique. Learn to pull through the clicker, not to it.

ANALYSIS

There is not and never will be a definitive description of what goes into the perfect archery technique. No two champion archers look exactly alike. Draw elbow height, the exact sequence of shot build-up, finger position on the string and similar physical characteristics will vary to some degree. Analysing the shot by those criteria probably does more harm than good. The archer himself is probably not even thinking about that particular aspect. He is far more likely to be checking the 'feel' of the shot, and concentrating on aim. Key words that ran through all the interviews were Control, Power, Line, Rhythm, Flow, Automation, Relax, Feel, Pressure, Pulling through, Extend, Tension and Consistency. Almost without exception they refer to how you control the sequence rather than what you do in the mechanical sense. And perhaps their strongly abstract nature reveals a clue to such high standards of performance – they are the building blocks of that elusive factor 'mental approach'.

Unfortunately, many years of misguided analysis have resulted in a pre-occupation among up-and-coming shooters and coaches with the bits and pieces of style rather than with the control aspect. They have dissected so many styles and techniques that only confusion remains, a case of paralysis by analysis. On top of that, things are not necessarily what they seem anyway; and as a result certain misconceptions are now firmly rooted in archery education. Take back tension and shoulder blades as an example.

There are very, very few archers who have not been taught that to shoot well they must concentrate on squeezing their shoulder blades together to produce back tension and to pull the arrow from under the clicker. Then why is it that you can stand all day on the line, back muscles tensed to the point of going into spasm, yet the damn clicker won't click? Quite simple really: the coaches who analysed shoulder blade action got it wrong.

Squeezing your shoulder blades together neither extends the draw nor produces back tension. The reverse is really the case: the correct use of the shoulders and back has the *effect* of squeezing the shoulder blades together to some extent. Mark

Blenkarne adds another dimension to the equation. He says that because of the extension of his bow shoulder towards the target, plus the powerful pull of his back muscles, both his shoulder blades are moving in the same direction. The feeling of squeezing is due to the rear shoulder blade moving faster and catching up with the front.

The significance of all this is not so much exactly what does what, but why. In the case of shoulder blades, you need to appreciate that the sensation of squeezing, pushing or whatever is a *result* of something else – in this case of getting the bow on to your back, then extending the pressure. Drawing up any old how, then deliberately squeezing your shoulder blades

together or having them play tag across your back is nowhere near the same thing.

To some degree, most of archery's traditional and unsuccessful coaching tactics are founded on equally muddled thinking. Having your draw hand recoil behind your neck after release is another example. You can deliberately snatch it back there. But really it is a reaction of the powerful back and shoulder muscles being suddenly freed from holding the weight of the bow. Again, a different matter entirely, an effect not a cause.

Misconceptions like these do not produce good results, yet they are still taught to thousands of archers as part of the basic coaching programme. Very few archers ever make rapid and sustained progress. One unfortunate spin-off is that these same archers become sceptical of any kind of advice and coaching, and eventually it becomes their natural reaction to conclude that good shooting is therefore based on very difficult principles that demand a lot of talent and a brain like Einstein's. I made the same mistake, and were it not for that first letter to Roy Matthews I would either be struggling without hope or, more likely, would by now have given up archery altogether.

The hardest lesson I learned, which producing this book has further reinforced, is that to make any serious progress in the sport the vast majority of archers must clear their minds of all the complication and mystique, and begin afresh with relatively simple thought patterns. If you have been shooting for a year or two, the probability exists that you know *too much* about technique, but you know *little or nothing* about mental attitude and control. It's a hard lesson to learn, and there is no kind way to put the message across.

The hardest part is to accept that the top archers have no earth-shattering secrets. Or are Roy Matthews and the rest all in league to confuse us? Well, you'll have to make up your own mind on that. But if you decide that they are holding something back, please answer this one. How did all those archers I talked to – many of whom don't even know each other – manage to come up with essentially the same explanation of how to shoot properly? Have they conspired to hoodwink us? Are they telepathic? Or are they simply telling the truth as they see it? As a matter of fact, that may lead you towards the most important question I asked myself while researching and editing this book. Are they being honest with me? Or do I find it hard to accept what they say because I have not been honest with myself about my own shooting?

11 Equipment in Perspective

Every archer knows that no bow can shoot arrows all by itself; yet often we kid ourselves into thinking otherwise. Discovering the truth sometimes costs years of frustration and a lot of hard cash besides. Just as there is no magic formula involved in the shooting of a bow, nor do bows, arrows and the rest of an archer's tackle hold any secrets of their own. Coming to terms with the situation is an important stage in developing the right skills and mental approach to shoot high scores.

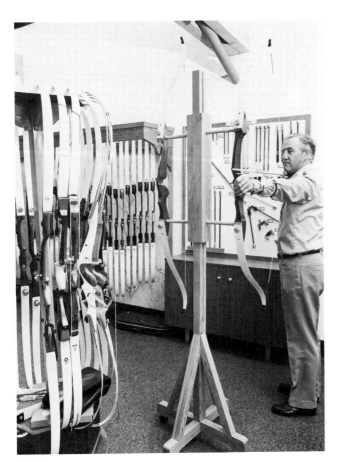

The tremendous range of quality equipment now available ensures that everyone can start the day's shooting on an equal footing.

Years ago this was not quite the case. Bows varied a great deal, even among samples of the same model. When arrows were handcrafted from wood, assembly and matching were critically important; so much so that a man with a magic touch could pick up points on the more hamfisted competitors. But today's precision-cast handles, limbs of advanced glassfibre and resin construction, drawn aluminium alloy shafts and points matched within a grain or so add up to an entirely different picture. Because archery equipment is so good and its performance so predictable, now the archer's shooting skill becomes the focal point. For the first time in the history of the sport the emphasis lies with the archer himself, and between shooters, scoreboard and record book. We all start the day equal, and the best man wins because he is best, not because his tackle is superior.

All well-designed bows built to high tolerances are as accurate as any other, in theory at least. Why then do champion archers tend to be loyal to one particular make? The reasons are subjective – they like shooting a particular bow. It somehow feels right, and they are more confident. Or a bit of commercial intrigue is involved: most high-ranking archers are provided with free equipment or enjoy specially subsidised prices. Only occasionally do you hear someone say, 'those Brand X bows are real junk. Won't shoot straight. My Supershot is without doubt the world's most accurate bow.' What they usually say is something along the lines of 'I've shot all the top bows, but I still prefer mine. If I wanted to, I could pick up more or less any bow and shoot good scores after a couple of hours' familiarisation and tuning. Yes, I would shoot better still with my own tackle, but that's mainly because I am so confident in it.'

How seldom you hear club archers talk that way. Usually it's a case of hankering after the latest bow to hit the market, the one that holds some world or national record or is shot by a respected archer of national or world class. It is amazing how many newcomers settle for the same brand as the club champion's. There are Yamaha-biased clubs, Hoyt brigades, Marksman strongholds. Without detracting from the bows in any way, this trend cannot be based on any logical choice. More likely, it is in the hope that something magic will rub off. So which bow should you shoot? In all probability the one you like the feel of the most will produce the best results. That is how champions choose their equipment.

BOW SELECTION

Researching the question of bow selection did produce two points worth putting under the microscope, one encouraging, the other frankly disturbing. Among Far

Filing out the string nocks.

British design and craftsmanship – Arten's Olympic sight on the slim, sculptured handle of Tony Preston's Perris Whitehart.

Eastern bows particularly, quality control has slipped. Bad limbs, misalignment between limbs and handle, stacking, draw weights way up or down on marked figures are among the leading complaints; and they are far, far more common than anyone could possibly deem acceptable even in a mass-produced item where quality control cannot rival that of handbuilt equipment. While in principle it is wrong to assume that changing to another make or model of bow will improve your scores, the fact remains that your own bow might be a runt from the litter. Do check for yourself, or have an experienced archer do it for you. Some errors are of no consequence or can be eliminated by tuning. Others cannot – and are the best reason in the world for buying a new bow.

The good news is that specialist bowyers are at last coming out of their shells and taking on the international companies with major success. Every country where bows are shot boasts at least one bowyer of

Laminating the wood and glassfibre components of a recurve limb.

Shaping a wooden Portland handle.

than half the price) yet they shoot every bit as well. It would appear that you are far less likely to get a bad one. The lesson is clear: don't be brainwashed into thinking that only one or two makes of bow can shoot world-class scores. The archers who set the records preferred their particular brand for largely subjective reasons; which is an entirely different matter from *having* to use it for performance's sake.

DRAW WEIGHT

Assuming that your bow is properly made, the important consideration is draw weight, with bow length, handgrip and other design features playing lesser roles. The rule of thumb for draw weight is

consequence. In Britain three spring immediately to mind (yet they are by no means the only ones). Border Bows, Marksman and Perris Archery between them offer a range of target and hunting recurves that equal the best performance the rest of the world can produce; and in finish, materials and workmanship are generally superior.

Archers sometimes shy away from buying bows which do not have an international reputation. It is difficult to say why. When prices are lower than those of a famous Japanese or American bow, does doubt arise about performance and quality? Is low price itself a deterrent? There should certainly be no worries on any score; British and European bows are truly superb by anyone's standards. In addition, British equipment prices have become formidably competitive since sterling's fall on the money markets.

The Perris Whitehart built by Tony Preston, and Marksman's Portland range cost far less than most imported big name bows (some models are little more

Quality control in action. Every Marksman handle, like those of the Perris and other leading British bows, is cast and finished to high standards of accuracy and performance.

Care and craftsmanship are the hallmark of specialist bow manufacturers. This Marksman hunting bow is virtually handmade.

Marksman's new KG 2000 features the latest in bow design but retains the age-old traditions of classic British bowyery.

mark point of view. For ladies and juniors the corresponding figures are lower, with 32–35lb (14–16kg) a ballpark figure for club-level shooting. Most international women shoot draw weights hardly above those figures, though there are one or two stronger women who rival the men.

Draw length must be carefully calculated. It is quite wrong to guess your arrow length, or to rely on one of the traditional measuring tricks such as finger tips to breastbone distance. Length is dictated by physique, technique and anchor point. If you don't know how to measure it, get experienced advice beforehand. Arrow length, spine and draw weight are interrelated, so without knowing them all you cannot be sure of buying the correct power and length of bow. Mistakes at this stage are very expensive, yet they are commonplace.

According to some coaches and retailers, many an archer takes it into his head that he needs to shoot a bow of certain draw weight or an arrow of a particular length and specification. It turns out that he is copying the set-up shot by some star performer, often an Olympic archer, world champion or somesuch hero. Crazy, but it does happen. To stand any chance of success you must shoot *your* correct draw weight, arrow length and spine rating. One would have thought that went without saying, but apparently it is far from the case. On most shooting lines you will see archers heavily overbowed and arms stretched to breaking point. Shooting 30in 2115s from a 50 pounder poses an irresistible challenge for some macho clubmen.

Concern about the wind and its effect on arrow performance and accuracy contributes hugely to the trend towards heavy bows and meaty arrows, and is probably what induces archers to take on too much draw weight. Theoretically, for any given velocity a heavy shaft will hold its path better than a light arrow. Because momentum is more important than arrow speed, a big, relatively slow moving shaft should comfortably outshoot a featherweight shaft that zips out of the bow. Pure speed is actually a deterrent to accuracy in rough conditions because air resistance increases dramatically in relation to rising velocity.

At the end of the day *control* makes the difference. Very often a lightly-bowed archer who stays in

basically to shoot as heavy a bow as you can *control* – bearing in mind that the last shot of a FITA round demands just as much care as the first. It is generally agreed that a heavier bow tends to compensate for release variations far more than does a lightly stressed string and limbs which are all too easily interfered with at the critical moment.

There is no correct poundage in the sense of a neat formula based on age, body weight, sex and height. Trial and error is the only way to discover exactly how much you can safely control. Also – a point in favour of the take-down bow with its easily interchangeable limbs – draw weight and arrow length will increase to some extent with experience. Around the 35lb (16kg) mark seems appropriate for the majority of adult male beginners; the average draw weight of international-grade men is between 45 and 50lb (20–23kg). Most experienced men can expect to end up somewhere in the middle ground, say 40–42lb (18–19kg) on the fingers, which is adequately powerful from the sight command will outscore a heavy-bowed but less competent shooter whose stamina is gone after the first three dozen shots. As in most areas of successful shooting, we come back to control being the decisive factor; and to achieve that you have to shoot equipment that suits you. Now and again you will come across a heavy tackle shooter who does stay in command and shoots the middle out of the target in stormforce winds while your equally well-shot arrows drift like autumn leaves. That's life.

OTHER FEATURES

Apart from the feel of the bow and its draw weight, most design features of modern recurves do not seem too important to top-grade shooting. Variable draw weight and tiller adjustment facilities are not considered to contribute very much to a bow's performance, although they can provide extra scope for tuning. Expert archers are more likely to question the stability and inherent accuracy of the bow once its limb bolts are adjusted. All right, so you can take the draw weight up by 10 per cent. In doing so you alter the limb/handle geometry – what effect does that have on grouping and ease of shooting?

Tillering adjustment prompts the same mildly cynical response. What can shifting tiller on a FITA recurve outfit achieve for the vast majority of archers that moving the nocking point cannot? Underlying

Les Howis, Britain's master bowyer, checks a batch of Portland limbs.

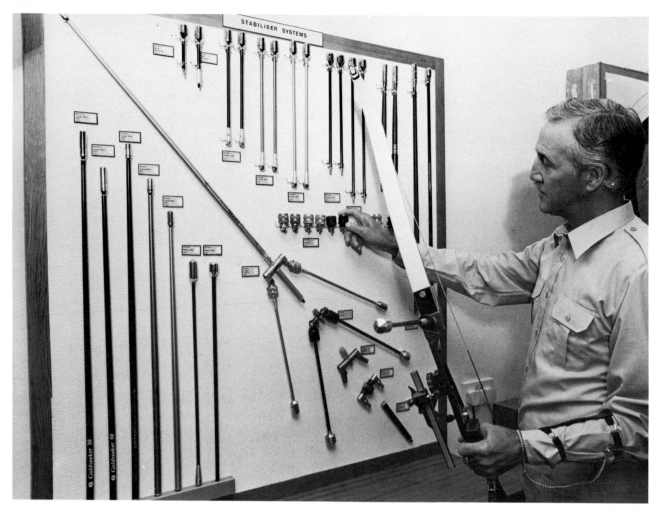

Stabilisation is really a question of trial and error.

these and related questions is a suspicion that in many cases those supposedly indispensable modern design features are largely cosmetic, or are the result of innovation for its own sake. Similar doubts surround the use of carbonfibre in bow limbs. The evidence that the way in which carbon is currently employed in limb construction makes any real difference to accurate shooting is flimsy. If one considers that the cost of the carbon cloth cannot possibly amount to much more than £3, how can such high prices be justified?

Ultimate accuracy depends far more on simple features like handgrip, pressure button and arrow rest. Most archers are aware of the various options, and certainly at top levels of shooting very few compromises are accepted. At stake here are those subjective elements of feel, confidence and control – key factors in success. However, since the majority of

these fittings and accessories can be changed at will, it really does not matter how the bow comes out of the factory. It is easy and often most beneficial to strip the handle bare and equip it according to preference.

Commercially produced buttons and rests are widely available and there is seldom any need to look further for impeccable performance. Handgrips are the one exception, since while interchangeable grips are usually available in high, medium and low wrist versions, they still may not produce the exact angle and feel that the archer insists upon. There is always the option either to modify a standard grip by carving away the plastic or wood, or to dispense with it and build up new grip from Plastic Padding or a similar resin-based filler.

Bow-sights are another area for personal preference. Because of their weight and balance some models do affect a bow's feel and will be rejected for that reason alone. On the whole, any high quality sight with a full range of adjustment is acceptable. Interchangeable sight-pins, apertures and inserts are very useful, particularly while the archer is still at the experimental stage. Variable extension is another useful feature if it is kept within sensible limits. All too often aiming becomes a pre-occupation to the detriment of the shot's execution. In seeking a more accurate sight picture by extending the sight-pin too far forward, the archer discovers that his shooting technique loses its edge.

Stabilisers are the final piece in the jigsaw, and what chaos they cause. Long rods, twins, V-bars . . . what is best, and where will it all end? Again it pays to look at it from the experienced archer's angle. Most really good archers confirm that no stabiliser system is tremendously superior to the rest. Made to shoot with a full V-bar set-up, then the long rod/twin stabiliser combination, and finally with just plain twins, the best archers would certainly maintain very high standards throughout, and it might be difficult to separate comparative scores by more than a few points. Even so, one particular combination would inspire the most confidence and thus provide that competitive edge.

Statistically speaking, the V-bar unit, long rod plus single stabiliser at the top of the handle is most popular among leading male international target archers. Perhaps due to its lighter weight, the long rod/twin stabiliser combination finds most addicts among the ladies. However, there are leading men who use long rod/twins, and by the same token more than a few women prefer the V-bar. For male archers at least, the V-bar has a slight technical advantage. The extra stability, weight and balance adjustment it affords really do pay off with heavy poundage bows and stiff arrows. Yet those benefits can backfire with low draw weights and smaller shaft sizes. Too much stabilisation can upset bow performance and tuning.

Perhaps the best explanation of stabilisation lies in the words of an internationally famous archer who told me that when he is shooting well, it doesn't matter what he uses. The arrows still go straight down the middle. By the same token, no particular combination compensates for poor form. So why does he use a V-bar? 'I like the way I can set it up to produce exactly the balance I prefer and the right reaction at release. And when I'm shooting pretty well, but not quite in top form, they certainly do cover up some mistakes and add a few extra points.'

The message is clear enough: try them all if necessary. Stabilisation is a very personal matter: from selection, to the way you tune it, even down to the amount of weight you attach to the rods. Even the setting of TFC pressure boils down to trial and error. Most keen archers already own enough bits and pieces to allow a free choice between the two main systems, so it costs nothing to run the necessary experiments. As a rough guide, heavier bows call for heavier weights and/or longer rods (though too much weight can stifle the bow's power); usually you can switch systems without radically retuning the bow, but some minor tweaking is always essential; and too much weight up front can cause the arrow to slap the handle or the arrow rest unless appropriate counterweights are screwed to the inside of the handle. Apart from that, stabilisation is not so much a science as an exercise in feel, balance and confidence – which brings us full circle to those important subjective elements that recur throughout the book. Top performers seem to prefer a simple approach – if the outfit feels right it will shoot right. And once you have found that basic setting all the experimentation in the world results in minor improvements at most. Stop worrying and start shooting!

12 Tuning

The way in which a bow, accessories, string and arrows are set up and tuned has a tremendous bearing on shot-by-shot consistency and grouping power. Expert archers take great care in getting it right. Unfortunately, the setting up and tuning process is responsible for a great deal of frustration in the lower ranks of tournament shooters. Quite a few do not really understand what the game is all about; and a surprising number who have studied tuning still cannot fathom out why the various techniques produce either the wrong results from their equipment or do not work at all.

To tune your tackle properly, you must be able to shoot well; but to shoot confidently and to develop your own personal style, the bow must be fairly well tuned. It is something of a Catch 22 situation. Perfection is when you know that any variation in arrow flight and grouping is *your* fault. Then the onus is on you to correct whatever weaknesses are creeping in. However, if it becomes a case of was it you, or is the bow at fault – which way do you jump?

Tuning and technique are variations on a theme, and they grow in parallel. The better you learn to shoot, the easier it is to tune the bow and the better the results will be. The immediate problem for new and intermediate archers is knowing where to make a start. Be realistic: whatever you do, don't waste time trying to achieve perfect results. Initial priorities are to make the bow shoot smoothly and quietly, and to achieve reasonably clean arrow release. Obviously you cannot shoot even remotely respectable groups if the shaft smashes against sight, arrow rest or bow handle.

Tuning makes an appreciable difference to a good archer's scoring power and it is therefore important to keep a check on your equipment as your technique improves. Something of a paradox may arise. Some excellent archers find that the better they shoot, the less important tuning becomes. Ultra-fine tuning produces neither tighter groups nor greater con-sistency. Others discover that their tackle responds dramatically – a tweak of the pressure button, a change of arrow rest or a variation in bracing height closes or opens their groups quite appreciably.

The best advice is to be aware of tuning but not hamstrung by it. Nevertheless, be aware that too casual an approach might cost you dearly. If, say, your arrows group within the red at 70 metres but you are fairly sure that your technique and control are more than good enough to produce higher scores, perhaps tackle

Tuning controls how the bow limbs inject the archer's muscle power into the arrow nock.

is to blame. A good many top archers consider that fine tuning at this stage could well halve group diameter and put a substantially higher proportion of arrows into the gold ring. They stress, too, that after being re-tuned the bow may feel no better, and may even feel slightly rougher. Results are seen at the target end only. No amount of fine tuning will put a 1000 shooter into the 1200 bracket, but an archer shooting low 1200s might pick up 25 points or more by refining his bow set-up and arrow flight pattern. Perfect arrow flight and tight groups are the result of:

1. Equipment matching – how bow, arrow, string and accessories interact with each other.
2. Technique and control – how you *personally* shoot the outfit.
3. Tuning – the technique of blending the above for best results.

Simply defined, a tuned outfit is one in which the archer's muscle power is channelled efficiently into the bow, then injected accurately into the arrow nock. The more precisely the power flows into the arrow, the less the shaft will deviate under acceleration, and the more cleanly it leaves the bow. Thus, the more quickly it settles onto its flight path and the less work the fletchings must do. As one archer put it, 'tuning means making the string hit the arrow straight up the backside'. A graphic description, and exactly right.

One might suppose that with today's advanced materials and manufacturing techniques, bows and arrows should come off the dealer's shelf pre-matched and perfectly tuned. If everyone shot the same way, that might be the case. The problem – and the reason we have to tune individually – is that because of their physical differences and varied styles, no two archers draw the bow and let go of the string in exactly the same way. A tuning combination that results in perfect arrow flight for one archer will be miles off for another.

This does not mean that tuning is a difficult process. In many cases everything necessary can be achieved within an hour or two. More important than what you do is when you do it – in other words you need a plan of campaign. Blindly shooting hundreds of arrows is no answer. First you tend to the basic set-up of bow, string, arrows, and so on. Second, you tune them to

Weigh the bow limbs at your personal draw length to assist in choosing the right arrow from the spine chart.

react properly to your personal style. Considered in these two stages, the work is easier and the results more predictable.

The basic archery set-up refers to bow, sight, stabilisers and accessories like pressure button and arrow rest. Almost without exception, the combination can be chosen to reflect the brand names, feel and quality you like. As previous chapters have outlined, there is little difference in performance between components such as various stabiliser systems, so unless you do anything outrageous there is no real reason to suppose that results will be less than excellent or that the tackle will fail to respond to standard tuning techniques.

Archers tend to forget that any *change* in the set-up will affect its tune. Adding stabiliser weights, lengthening rods, swapping arrow rests all affect the arrow's response. Mostly the effects are minor, perhaps too small to worry about or even to detect. Sometimes, though, you will need to make a significant

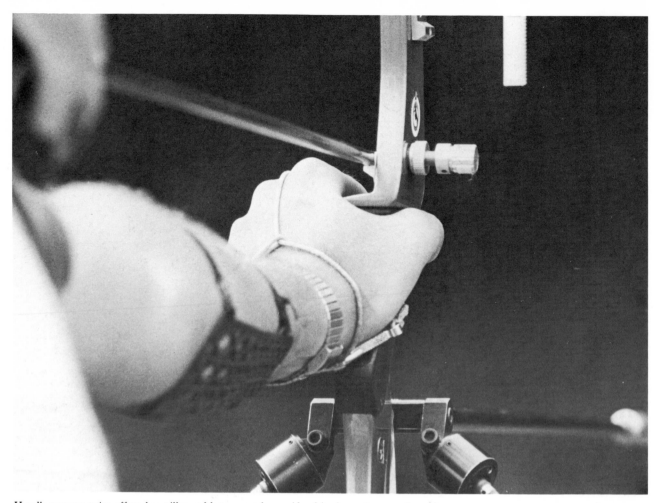

Handle pressure point affects bow tiller and hence must be considered in the tuning equation.

change in bracing height, degree of centre shot, button pressure or even shaft selection; or you will find that straying too far from standard set-up produces an untunable outfit – particularly if the stabiliser system becomes too heavy and imbalanced. The rule is simple enough: change the set-up, check the tuning.

STRINGS

Strings, so boring compared to bows and the other goodies, are overlooked by the majority of archers who shoot modest scores. Most high-scoring archers are almost neurotic about theirs. The string, they claim, is at least as important as the bow and arrows and must be seriously considered in its own right. Make them yourself or have them custom-made by somebody who

really knows what he's doing.

There is nothing complicated about a bow string, of course. Endless loop strings and laid-in strings are equally efficient and long-lasting if wound and served with care. The trouble with mass-produced strings is that they tend to vary too much in quality and specification. Some are served loose, others too tight. Most strings lie somewhere within the bow's bracing height range, but seldom will you find two or three in a batch that are *exactly* the same. Even a quarter inch brace height variation upsets fine tuning. Twisting or untwisting the string allows for some adjustment, but even the number of twists affects the string's performance and consistency.

Most of today's bow limbs are designed to withstand the shock and stress of shooting non-stretch Kevlar and as a result will not produce anywhere near as high a performance with the older string materials. This is an important point to consider when buying strings – you may no longer have the option of shooting Dacron and getting good results. Kevlar is more consistent and more efficient than Dacron but it does not last as long, and that is what worries many an archer of the old school. It is not a problem once you accept that Kevlar strings have a relatively short lifespan – are a disposable commodity in other words. Instead of trying to wring a year's shooting from a string, throw it away after a thousand shots. Any reasonably well made Kevlar string lasts that long with ease, and it does not have to be specially served and lubricated. Ordinary twisted nylon servings, even monofilament, are

perfectly satisfactory. The cost is minimal if you make your own. Time? Anyone can make an endless loop string in half an hour; laid-in strings are even quicker. And apart from anything else, your strings can all be the right length, which is of enormous value in maintaining your bow's tune over a long period.

Most people understand the relationship between string length, bracing height and tuning. String *weight* is almost as important. The number of strands (and thereby the string's weight) recommended by the bowyer provide a satisfactory performance; even so, remember that the energy unleashed by the recoiling bow limbs drives the *combined* weights of string and arrow. If you shoot a light arrow (light relative to the

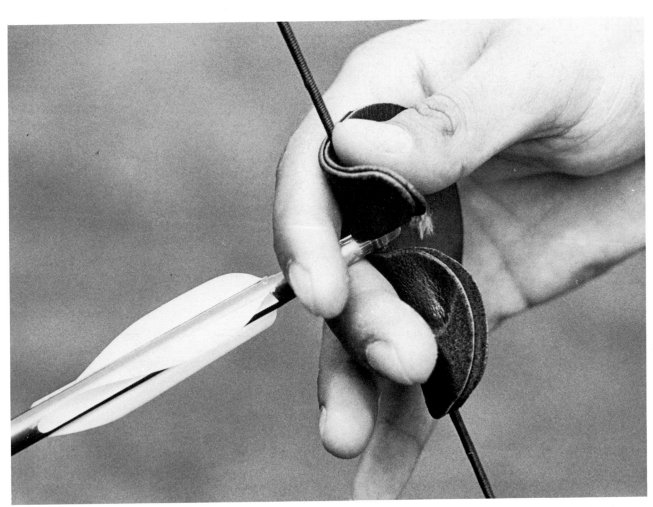

Tillering variations caused by finger size and pressure are the main reason why nocking point is so important in successful arrow launch.

bow's draw weight, that is), the bow may become more stable and quieter if string weight is increased. Conversely a heavy arrow can be pepped up by lightening the string and thus transferring more power to the shaft. Some experiment with strings plus or minus two strands from standard may produce interesting results.

The nocking point's position has a profound effect on arrow flight, and its *structure* also is important. Arrow nocks that fit too tightly will tune differently from normal; if the nock skids because it sits too loosely on the string, that too will influence the tuning process. Over-large nocking points foul the tab as the string is released. Dental floss, metal rings and shrink-on sleeves are all satisfactory nocking point components if used with care, but for first class results and versatility it is hard to beat cotton thread soaked in superglue. A blob of hardened cotton holds the arrow at the correct nocking height, and the string can be built up to fit snugly inside the nock slot.

ARROWS

Today's aluminium alloy arrows are remarkably tough and reliable. Equally important in target shooting, they offer tremendous versatility in length, point specification, spine and fletching. Gone is the traditional archer's worry about matching shaft spine exactly to the bow's weight. The manufacturer's selection charts, though still an excellent basis for matching, are open to liberal interpretation. Pressure buttons, flipper rests and bow handles cut well past centre-shot offer such versatility of tuning that you can shoot virtually any grade of shaft – within reasonable limits of course. In some respects the only limitation is whether you can achieve a realistic sight mark at 90 metres (70 metres for the women's FITA).

The shaft or shafts recommended by spine selection charts generally prove satisfactory for your bow and the way you shoot it, and archers new to the sport do well to look no further until they gain some experience of shooting and tuning. But while there are no miracles involved in shifting from those basic guidelines, still there are distinct advantages that could repay a little investigation.

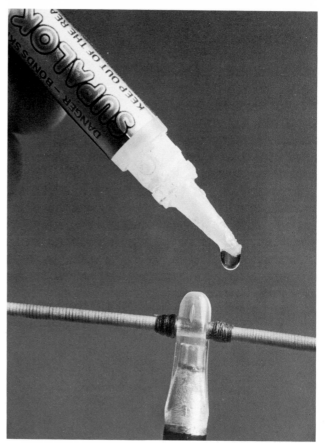

Nocking points built up from cotton thread soaked in superglue are accurate and long lasting.

If a bow were 100 per cent efficient, every ounce of energy stored in its limbs at full draw would be transferred to the arrow and string upon release. But bows are not perfect, nor are they all identical. A 40lb (18kg) weapon might shoot an arrow faster than another model that also weighs 40lb at full draw. Archers also vary: six men shooting the same bow would produce six different arrow speeds.

Spine charts are based on average bows and average archers – and that is why they are accurate enough most of the time. For any given draw weight, there will always be exceptions. The 'right' arrow will prove too whippy or too stiff due to variations in bow efficiency and the archer's personal technique. Mostly, tuning will prove reasonably corrective, but surprisingly often it does not result in the very best performance.

As bow design becomes more sophisticated, simple selection charts that list just one recommendation for each arrow length and 5–10lb (2·2–4·5kg) draw weight band do not prove quite accurate enough. At the very least, consult the full Easton comparator where you can work in half inch increments and down to the nearest pound of draw weight. In addition, the stiffness/weight relationship of one shaft to another is accurately illustrated. If you think a slightly stiffer shaft of virtually the same weight would shoot better, you can select it by direct comparison on paper.

Highly efficient modern bow limbs, Kevlar and heavy stabilisation distort the chart's accuracy. While the standard shaft suggested will certainly shoot fairly well, there is a great deal to be said for routinely choosing the next stiffer grade of shaft. It will prove to be a better match, and being stiffer tends to iron out some mistakes as well. Stiffer shafts are more forgiving of release error, so what little you may lose in arrow speed is more than offset by higher consistency and hence tighter groups.

The quest for speed certainly creates problems for many archers. In theory a fast-flying arrow has advantages, but in practice the only benefit lies in the sight mark. Apart from gaining a few millimetres in this department, the outcome of tuning aluminium alloy shafts purely for speed is all bad. Shooting a much lighter than normal arrow leads to a marked lack of stability. There is no forgiveness of error in technique, and the shaft is fighting the string and the bow. Tuning is more critical and the fletching must work extremely hard.

Champion archers are not unduly concerned about

Draw length and arrow length must be determined by experiment and ideally with a coach's assistance. It is no good simply guessing.

high arrow speeds. Forgiveness, tight grouping and easy tuning are considered far more important than an extra few feet per second. Technical data on leading archers' equipment almost without exception shows arrow speed to be quite modest, especially among the higher ranking performers. In many cases the arrow grade selected is at least one step stiffer than chart recommendation. One or two of the world's very best shooters actually raise the bow's bracing height in order to provide better clearance for a very stiff shaft. Shortening the string itself slows down the arrow, but presumably the trade-off between lower speed and higher stability is considered a valuable investment.

Carbonfibre/aluminium shafts introduce a new concept. Carbonfibre's immense stiffness produces an arrow that is much slimmer and lighter than an aluminium shaft of equivalent spine. The new shafts leave the bow at significantly higher velocity. Thus, Space Age technology enables an archer to gain speed while retaining the forgiveness that adequate shaft stiffness provides. Are carbonfibre/aluminium arrows the answer to every shooter's prayers? Having been shot to world record levels, they certainly prove most effective in the right hands. But there is no reason to suppose that they offer any measurable advantage to the vast majority of archers, including most internationals. Until these new shafts cost a lot less than the current £200 a set, few archers are likely to take any gambles on finding out for themselves.

Though much less expensive than carbon/aluminium, even X7s alloy arrows are a big investment. Is their cost justified? Considering how well they last, they may work out more economical than XX75s in the long run; or so some archers claim. However, it is a mistake to assume that XX75s are inevitably less *accurate*. For that matter, there is no real disadvantage in shooting the latest Sherwood and Sonic shafts which cost less than even the cheapest Easton tubing.

Straightness, weight and consistency of spine are important considerations which on paper at least give the highest quality shafts a distinct advantage over lesser grade tubing. But according to several authorities on archery tackle, the technical specifications are somewhat meaningless in everyday shooting, and may be of limited significance at championship levels as well. Perfect straightness is

desirable but not absolutely essential: a deviation of up to 0·004in per foot is said to have no measurable effect on an archer's group. A few grains variation in weight of shaft or point will have no visible effect at the target, not even at 90 metres. However, really cheap shafts can be ruled out because they do not offer a large enough range of sizes, and in some cases are markedly prone to bending. Keen archers will therefore choose between X7s, XX75s and the latter's close equivalents like Sonic and Sherwood.

Given a choice between two shafts of reasonably similar stiffness but different weights, the majority of archers discover that the lighter wall shaft will shoot a little bit better; 2014s or 2114s generally can be expected to outdo 2016s, for instance. However, this is not invariably so, and it is up to the archer to run his

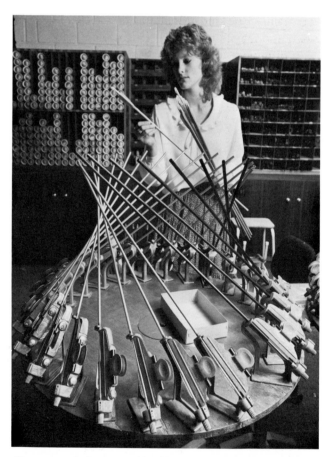

Most arrow shafts are capable of high performance, and you can sometimes save a lot of money by picking an economical grade instead of X7s. Spine charts are accurate enough for beginners but may not indicate the perfect shaft for a more experienced archer.

own tests. The same applies to heavy and regular weight points. Despite the various pros and cons advanced on the subject of shaft balance and point design, the fact remains that what suits one archer might not prove satisfactory for another. There is no clear-cut advantage in using a heavy pointed arrow; and in an individual archer's case there could well be a very good reason not to use them – namely, groups are tighter with a standard point.

Owing to metallurgical differences in the various grades and makes of shaft, some archers find that XX75s give better results than X7s, or vice versa. The answer probably lies in the harmonic pattern of the shaft as it accelerates past the bow. An arrow's response to being punched by the string varies not only with its spine rating and weight, but also in the crystalline structure of the aluminium alloy itself. Sometimes one kind of shaft just happens to harmonise with an archer's technique. It is not going to make a vast difference, but might mean a few extra points for archers already shooting high scores.

Fletchings stabilise the arrow during its initial oscillatory phase, then steer it through the remainder of its flight. The more cleanly the arrow leaves the bow, and the less oscillations occur (in other words, the better the matching and tuning) the less work the fletchings must do, and in a perfect world tiny vanes would be enough. However, in real life it pays to add good stabilisation in the form of realistically large vanes – in the order of 2–2½in (50–60mm) for 28–29in (71–74cm) shafts, proportionately smaller for lighter, shorter arrows.

Fletchings also enhance accuracy and stabilisation by spinning the shaft along its axis. Ordinary flat plastic vanes must be slightly offset to generate the necessary twist. A two or three degree angle of attack suits most arrows, and the spin is further developed by using a reasonably rigid material. Extremely soft vanes are best avoided for that reason. To avoid the possibility of the arrow striking the rest or bow handle, the vanes should spin the shaft clockwise for a right-handed archer (looking at it from the nock end).

Like most other archery equipment, vanes come in all shapes and sizes. Provided you stick to a size in keeping with the arrow's length and stiffness, there is no reason to believe that any particular brand or profile

Provided they are no more than 0.004in/ft out of true, arrow shafts will be perfectly accurate.

of vane excels. Pick the style you like, clean the shaft, apply good quality glue and use an accurate fletching jig; those are the rules.

In America especially, big hunting-grade feathers are quite commonly used for indoor shooting. The idea is to impose so much drag that shaft vibrations are killed instantly. Greater accuracy results from the stability of the shaft alone, and is further enhanced by the nature of feathers themselves, which are particularly forgiving of an archer's mistakes.

Correctly fletched and nocked (the latter a formality provided the nocks are of high quality and the shaft swaging clean and undamaged) all modern arrow shafts offer extreme accuracy and long service life. However, it is unlikely that every arrow you fletch during your archery career, or buy ready made, will be perfect. Now and again there will be a rogue in the set. All leading archers are on the lookout for this shaft which somehow does not live up to expectations.

Sometimes an arrow consistently strays from the

group – perhaps it hits a few inches high and to the left. Generally, stripping off the nock and vanes then replacing them brings the shaft back into line. Occasionally it does not. The shaft weighs the same as the others, is perfectly straight and seems to be of equal spine rating. The reason remains a mystery, but the shaft is still a menace. Throw it away.

TUNING METHODS

So many pages of archery books and magazines are devoted to bow tuning that few archers involved in the sport for more than a couple of years are unaware of the various tuning methods available. In essence, they are all simple to carry out. Centre shot adjustment, button calibration and bracing height hold no great secrets and certainly do not demand a degree in engineering to understand.

As with shooting itself, most problems stem from placing too much emphasis on technicality and not enough on its everyday application. Rather than rehash a great deal of information that has been published many times before, this chapter seeks to look behind the pure mechanics of tuning to reveal some practical pathway through the maze of available information. Most of us seek little more than to learn about our own personal equipment; we are none too worried about becoming experts on the subject. A simple, commonsense path from A to B will do nicely.

New bows demand that you begin with some very simple tests which are a vital prelude to full-scale tuning. Beginners and relatively inexperienced archers cannot expect to take any short cuts, and even highly competent shooters with a lot of tuning knowledge under their belts still prefer to begin with the basics because they are such an essential foundation to return to if things go wrong.

Once you have fathomed out the equipment's characteristics, maintaining high performance is normally a matter of occasionally re-running whichever of the fine-tuning exercises you prefer. Nor is it always necessary to go right back to the start if, for example, you alter stabilisation, experiment with a slightly higher bracing height or switch to heavyweight piles. Fine-tuning tends to be self-

Clean the shafts with acetone or MEK, use a good quality adhesive, and set the vanes on the shaft at a 2–3 degree offset so that the arrow spins in flight.

diagnostic to some extent – the pattern of arrow hits reveals exactly what needs correcting, if anything.

Suppose you normally shoot 2014s tuned so that bare shaft and fletched arrows impact at the same point at 20 yards (18 metres), but you want to try out 2114s. The heavier bare shaft hits left of the fletched group, and a shade lower. This confirms what you know already – 2114s are stiffer than 2014s. Now you can re-tune the bow to bring that shaft back into the main group by altering the pressure button, shifting the nocking point, changing the bracing height, or whatever else it takes. There is no need to repeat the complete tuning programme.

PRELIMINARY TESTS

There is nothing so disconcerting as jumping in at the deep end, but tuning offers no alternative. Bow and arrows are not pre-matched and tuned in the factory, and it is up to you to find out exactly how they react to your shooting technique. Champion archers who were questioned about tuning tended to skip over these preliminaries; most of them have been shooting for so long that the horror of having to tune their equipment for the first time had faded from mind. However, after thinking about the subject for a moment they all came up with much the same suggestions about getting started.

1. Set the bracing height somewhere within the top half of its recommended range.
2. Fix an adjustable nocking point on the string so that the *bottom* of the plastic nock sits about ¼in (6mm) above square. (Dental floss or sticky tape will do for the nocking point.)
3. Pre-load the button to about 20oz (567g) – measured by pressing the button against household scales.
4. Screw the button into the handle and adjust it so that the arrow lies just left of centre-shot. Judge this by eye after lining up the string with the centre of the limbs as a datum point. A figure of ⅛–¼in (3–6mm) offset at the arrow point is suggested. Very few archers recommended that the arrow be set exactly on centre-shot. Most warned against it, saying that they found it almost impossible to tune a bow that way.

A thin coating of spray-on talcum powder reveals the slightest touch of arrow against bow.

Authorities on bow tuning say that the button's amount of centre shot must be determined before the spring pressure is adjusted from its basic setting of about 20oz for bows in the 40lb bracket, or about 15oz for lighter weapons.

Shoot a few dozen arrows at close range, more to check on how the bow feels than how tightly it groups. Time to familiarise yourself with the feel and reaction of the bow is judged very important. One or two high-scoring archers went even further: don't even attempt to tune the bow until you have shot for three or four days. That may be an extreme view, but the philosophy is sound enough. You cannot properly tune a bow unless you know its basic character and can control it.

No adjustment at this stage can be perfect, so over-enthusiastic attempts are sure to fail. Tuning is a systematic process of hacking into shape, knocking off the rough corners, then polishing. First consider the bow's sound and feel. Is it smooth and quiet, or does it clatter and judder? Provided arrows and string weight are reasonably well matched to the bow, and the basic adjustments are set fairly accurately, smoothness is largely the province of bracing height. Twist and untwist the string to adjust its length, and run up and down the bracing height range to determine where the bow shoots best. In all probability, the higher the brace height the smoother the bow shoots. Guard against going below the minimum figure recommended by the bowyer because to do so risks damaging string and limbs. On the whole, a high(ish) bracing height is kinder to the bow and promotes clean arrow clearance.

Perhaps the bracing height is not to blame. Sometimes an arrow hits the rest, bow handle or even the sight bar hard enough to be heard and felt. Plasticine around the button, a sprinkling of powder, or lipstick smeared on shaft, vanes and bow will reveal the tell-tale marks of a wayward arrow. Mark Blenkarne offered an interesting alternative: coat the rear of the arrow with spray-on talcum powder. A thin, absolutely even layer of powder pin-points every contact point, even the tiniest flicker of shaft against arrow rest.

Remember that you are looking for a real clash between bow and arrow, not a slight brushing of vane or shaft. These can be dealt with later, and will probably be corrected by the rest of the tuning programme anyway. Whipcracks and arm-wrenching vibrations are what we aim to eliminate. Bear in mind also that sometimes in the rush to tune a new bow obvious mistakes are overlooked. Perhaps the bow shoots badly because the string is hitting your chest, or your tab is worn out, or the arrow nocks are much too tight on the string. Does the handgrip not suit your style and thus generates excessive torque? Check everything before you blame the bow. However, most of the time bracing height will turn out to be the answer.

A smooth shooting bow and reasonable arrow clearance are great confidence boosters that set the scene for the real tuning process. However, it is still a mistake to think about fine tuning at this point. All you know is that the arrow does not go berserk when the string pushes it. There is a lot more to discover.

Badly tuned arrows can flirt off in any direction, but essentially they deviate up and down or from side to side. Some archers call it porpoising and fishtailing. Up and down problems are largely − but not exclusively − due to nocking point placement; side to side reactions are due to centre-shot, button pressure, arrow stiffness, stabilisers . . . a pretty long list. At the higher levels of tuning it is not quite so black and white. The two factors are inter-related; adjustment made in one plane affects the other to some degree. But at this stage life is much sweeter if you think of them as being independent. Of the two, vertical deviation is by far the most critical aspect of preliminary tuning and *must* be adjusted first. Unless the nocking point is within about ⅛in (3mm) of being spot on, more advanced tuning is a waste of time.

Nocking point location is best judged by shooting bare and fletched shafts at 15–20 yards (14–18m) and comparing their impact heights. However, a word of caution. Unless the nocking point and centre-shot settings are somewhere within tune when you run that test, the bare shaft will bend or even snap. Prevent that by roughly tuning a bare shaft at about three yards, then gradually working backwards. Shoot several times at each distance to determine the overall trend (sometimes the weave of the straw gives a false strike

The Arrowmeter is a useful check check on arrow speed. Some dealers provide this service for their customers because it does allow an instant assessment of shaft performance. However, most archers agree that pure speed reduces accuracy and consistency of shooting.

pattern) and aim so that the shaft lies parallel to the ground and points directly towards the boss.

You are interested in how the arrow strikes relative to horizontal and vertical. Angling downward (nock end high) indicates a high nocking point. Upward means the nocking point is too low. Nocks left or right suggest that the arrow is trying to plane off to one side or the other. Sometimes the pattern indicates an apparent fault in both planes – for instance, a high, left nock.

Adjust the nocking point until the shaft strikes close to horizontal. There is no need to be too fussy; this is not a fine tuning exercise. Now, small adjustments of the pressure button's centre-shot should iron out the worst side-to-side deviations. Again, don't expect miracles. Why not alter button pressure rather than centre-shot? The consensus of champion archers is this: it is better to preset the button to a fairly high tension and then rely on centre-shot adjustment for all but fine tuning. In their experience, correcting what could be major problems of tuning with spring pressure alone is certain to end in disaster.

Now increase the range by a couple of paces and repeat the test. The pattern will have altered to some extent, but do not jump to conclusions. There are two factors involved: untoward deviation of the shaft caused by lack of tuning or arrow mismatch; and the *normal* oscillation of the arrow as it leaves the bow and settles into steady flight. All shafts flicker to some degree during the first few yards. Is the arrow starting to go out of control? That is all you need to know.

In all probability, the original adjustments need little or no tweaking to keep the shaft reasonably on line. Any alterations are likely to involve centre shot rather than nocking height. Repeat the exercise until you are 15 yards (14m) from the boss. Provided the arrow is reasonably matched to the bow, the tuning process so far is merely a formality. Its aims are to establish a basic rapport between bow and arrow and – even more important – to prevent damaged arrows.

As you increase the range, major problems *gradually* make themselves felt. The shaft develops a will of its own. Nocking point adjustment works fairly well, but no amount of centre-shot alteration prevents the shaft diving left or right. By about ten yards (nine metres) it is obviously unwise to carry on – the shafts are so stiff

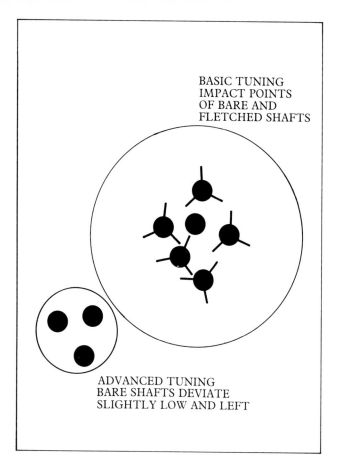

BASIC TUNING
IMPACT POINTS
OF BARE AND
FLETCHED SHAFTS

ADVANCED TUNING
BARE SHAFTS DEVIATE
SLIGHTLY LOW AND LEFT

DIAGRAM A   COMPARATIVE TUNING PATTERNS

or soft that further tests are not only invalid but are highly likely to damage the tubing. Far too many shafts – most of them brand new – are irretrievably damaged by archers who begin shooting at 15 yards (14m) or more with untuned or seriously incompatible tackle. Snapping an X7 first shot is no joke.

COMPARATIVE TUNING

This exercise, sometimes called the Bare Shaft Planing Test, has rapidly gained popularity. The principle is very simple. The basic idea of tuning is to inject the limb's energy straight into the nock, so that the arrow shaft accelerates exactly along its centre line. Provided its spine stiffness is within suitable limits, the shaft will clear the bow and fly cleanly. Up to about 20 yards (18m), fletchings are unnecessary – the impact point of bare and fletched shafts will be the same; in other words, they group together.

If the bow is not so accurately tuned, the fletched shaft still flies quite well, but the bare shaft will deviate because limb energy feeds in a little off-centre – high or low, one side or the other, or a mixture of both. By comparing where the two shafts lie in the target, you can determine where the problem lies; and by repeating the test you can monitor the effect of any adjustments. The basic idea is to bring the bare and fletched shafts back into one group.

Excellent descriptions of the technique appear in *Bow Tuning* by Roy Matthews (available from good archery shops or direct from the publishers, Marksman) and in Ed Eliason's section of Fred Bear's *World of Archery* (published by Doubleday). Fundamentally, tuning is a question of adjusting nocking height and button to correct horizontal and vertical deviation, but this time by comparing bare and fletched shafts rather than analysing the angle at which the shaft hits the boss. Fifteen yards (14m) is a good range to work from.

The basic rules are:

Bare shaft hits high – nocking point is too low.
Bare shaft hits low – nocking point is too high.
Bare shaft hits left – shaft is too stiff. Reduce button pressure, adjust centre-shot to bring arrow point further to the right, or both.
Bare shaft hits right – shaft is too soft. Increase pressure, move centre-shot adjustment to the left, or both.

Always correct the nocking point setting first, then look at the sideways deviation. You will find also that adjusting one plane affects the other to some degree, so be prepared to jiggle around with the settings to some extent.

Champion archers generally rely heavily on this planing shaft test for establishing the correct nocking point. It is the *only* way to assess and adjust it, they say. Comparative vertical impact is a firm indication of how well the arrow clears the bow, but more important it compares the tillering of the limbs to the archer's physique and style. Because the string grip determines how the limbs bend in relation to each other, tiller reaction is affected by fat or thin fingers, how string pressure is balanced between the three fingers, release characteristics, and so on. So there is far more at stake than adjusting the string to the arrow alone; nocking position is probably the most critical link between an archer and his bow.

Most experts recommend that the bow should initially be adjusted to bring bare and fletched shafts to the same impact point. The next step is to shoot the bow at normal FITA ranges to see how well it groups, how forgiving it is, and how it feels in general. For a good many archers, however, that first tune-up will not be quite right. If you prefer the planing system, the recommendation is to run some experiments in which the bare shaft is tuned to hit a short distance outside the main fletched group.

It is generally agreed that standard tuning falls down when you become tired towards the end of a round, or when you are not shooting quite as well as usual. In those circumstances, re-tuning the arrow to react slightly stiff and the nocking point to lie fractionally high seems to provide a very useful amount of forgiveness, and even in perfect circumstances may tighten groups at all distances. How much to alter the bow depends on the individual archer, but the most popular recommendation is to take the bare shaft somewhere towards the seven or eight o'clock position relative to the main group. At 20 yards (18m) the bare shaft should hit somewhere about 3in (7·6cm) low and up to 6in (15·2cm) left. The extra lift from the higher nocking point provides a shade more clearance at the back of the shaft, plus slightly more 'bounce' against the arrow rest to promote better forgiveness on the bad shots. By reacting more stiffly, the shaft also clears better and counteracts mistakes to some extent.

WALK-BACK TUNING

The planing shaft test offers a very sound solution to most tuning problems. Few archers need anything better in terms of tuning precision, and even world class competitors may be satisfied. Even so, there are two weaknesses in the technique. Firstly, when the bare shaft hits to one side of the fletched group, it is extremely difficult to know whether the button pressure is at fault, or if the degree of centre-shot needs altering instead. While shaft corrections can usually be made either way, you cannot be sure if you have made the right choice; and inevitably there are occasions when *both* are wrong.

Secondly, a perfectly tuned arrow still oscillates as it leaves the bow, and in some cases does not settle down for at least 20 yards. During that time it flickers left and right, up and down. Not enough to throw it off course, perhaps, but still by a detectable amount. Owing to the harmonic rhythms involved, you will find that tuning the tackle for 100 per cent results at 15 yards (14m) does not produce the same impact pattern at 10 or 20 yards (9 or 18m). So how do you know which is correct?

Walk-back tuning answers both questions. Arrow performance is examined at regular stages throughout the first 35 yards (32m) of flight. The technique

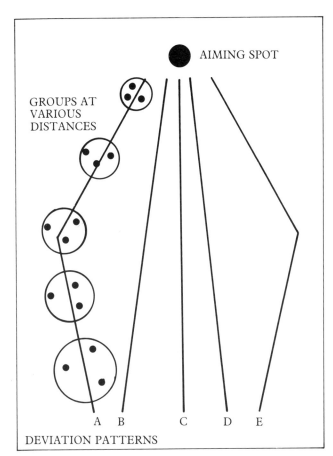

AIMING SPOT

GROUPS AT VARIOUS DISTANCES

A B   C   D E

DEVIATION PATTERNS

DIAGRAM B WALK BACK TUNING PATTERNS

involves shooting an arrow, walking back a few yards then shooting another . . . and so on. The sight-pin is not altered, and the aiming point stays the same. Thus the arrows form a vertical line down the target face. The pattern they make shows what adjustments are necessary, and the real bonus is that you can see the relationship between centre-shot and button pressure.

The exact distances chosen are quite unimportant. Most archers familiar with the technique shoot at 10, 15, 20, 25, 30 and 35 yards (or metres). A few extremely good shooters say that most oscillations can be narrowed down to a relatively small band within the 10–35 yard range. Having discovered where it is, they magnify that portion of the arrow's flight path by running new tests at, say, 12, 14, 16, 18, 20 and 22 yards. However, that step comes later – assuming it becomes necessary at all – and is definitely not recommended for inexperienced shooters.

Roy Matthews goes into detail in *Bow Tuning*, and it serves no useful purpose to bring in too much technicality here. The adjustments made to the bow are self-evident anyway once you can recognise the patterns produced on the target.

Refer to Diagram B.
1. Line A – too much spring pressure.
2. Line B – the button lies too far to the left.
3. Line C – perfect tuning.
4. Line D – the button lies too far to the right.
5. Line E – not enough button pressure.

A note of caution. Expert archers talk of shooting one arrow at each distance. They can get away with it because their groups are very tight. If you cannot shoot that well, shoot at least three arrows at each range then draw a circle around the group. Disregard obviously bad shots. Use the circles to analyse the strike pattern. The object is to produce a vertical row of groups. Be realistic though: an absolutely perpendicular line is fine in theory but very difficult to achieve in practice.

Even the diagnostic patterns may be less than perfect.

Sometimes the line appears to indicate a mixture of pressure and centre-shot error . . . a snake-like pattern emerges. The trick is not to adjust both parts of the button at once; that leads to even more confusion. Increase the *pressure* until the line straightens or assumes a definite indication of too much adjustment, from which you can work back. If now the line runs vertically down the target, fine. If not, alter the centre-shot to correct its sideways bias. Remember though, unless your shooting is of a very high standard absolutely regular patterns and straight lines are hard to achieve. Be realistic in your interpretation.

Walk-back tuning is quick and easy because the arrow pattern tells you exactly what to adjust. It has already replaced older tuning techniques to some extent and will probably become the target shooter's standard method. But it cannot analyse nocking height. For that you do need to compare a fletched and bare shaft.

ULTRA-FINE TUNING

By now your bow will be shooting extremely well, and even at high levels of competition there is no real need to do more work. However, there is another interesting angle to explore if you want to. Let's call it the 'what if' theory. What if I adjust the pressure button a fraction of an inch to the left? What if I take up the bracing height another ¼ in? What if button pressure is backed off half a turn? All you do is make the adjustment and shoot to see the effect, which is measured by feel, forgiveness and grouping power at medium-long range. Archers keen on the idea recommend 50 or 70 metres, and they confirm that sometimes these minor changes will pull in the groups. It is not a rational exercise, so there are no rules. And you need to be a real hotshot to gain any benefit.